THE *Dad* IN THE
MIRROR

Books by Patrick Morley

Coming Back to God
The Dad in the Mirror (coauthored with David Delk)
Devotions for Couples
Devotions for the Man in the Mirror
Discipleship for the Man in the Mirror
The Man in the Mirror
Second Half for the Man in the Mirror
Seven Seasons of the Man in the Mirror
Ten Secrets for the Man in the Mirror
Understanding Your Man in the Mirror
The Young Man in the Mirror

Books by David Delk

The Dad in the Mirror (coauthored with Patrick Morley)
Twists of Fate

THE Dad IN THE MIRROR

HOW TO SEE YOUR HEART FOR GOD REFLECTED IN YOUR CHILDREN

PATRICK MORLEY
DAVID DELK

ZONDERVAN™

GRAND RAPIDS, MICHIGAN 49530 USA

ZONDERVAN™

The Dad in the Mirror
Copyright © 2003 Patrick Morley and David Delk

Requests for information should be addressed to:

Zondervan, *Grand Rapids, Michigan 49530*

Library of Congress Cataloging-in-Publication Data

Morley, Patrick M.
  The dad in the mirror : how to see your heart for God reflected in your children /
Patrick Morley and David Delk.—1st ed.
    p. cm.— (The man in the mirror library)
  Includes bibliographical references.
  ISBN 0-310-25073-0
  1. Fathers—Religious life. 2. Fatherhood—Religious aspects—Christianity.
3. Parenting—Religious aspects—Christianity. I. Delk, David. II. Title. III. Series.
BV4529.M646 2003
248.8'421—dc21
                                                                        2003011383

The website addresses recommended throughout this book are offered as a resource to you. These websites are not intended in any way to be or imply an endorsement on the part of Zondervan, nor do we vouch for their content for the life of this book.

Published in association with the literary agency of Wolgemuth & Associates, Inc.

Interior design by Beth Shagene

Printed in the United States of America

---

03 04 05 06 07 08 09 /❖ DC/ 10 9 8 7 6 5 4 3 2 1

To my daughter, Jen, and her husband, Jay Simmons.
Jen, I have loved every minute of being your father.
You are so special, and that makes me proud. Jay, you are
the perfect husband for this effervescent woman.

PATRICK MORLEY

Ironically, even though this is a book on fathering,
I'd like to dedicate it to my mother, Janet Delk. In these
pages you will read about my father, but neither he nor I
would be who we are without a godly wife and mother.
Mom, in so many ways you laid down your life for me.
In the process you helped build a foundation of faith in
Christ. There are not enough words to say all that could
be said, so I'll settle for this: I love you.

DAVID DELK

Contents

Acknowledgments

We would like to acknowledge the host of wonderful pastors, authors, and teachers whose thoughts and ideas have impacted our thinking and lives. Their exact words may not appear in this book, yet they have shaped the worldview from which we write.

Pat would like to especially thank Patsy for being such a faithful sounding board, as well as his pastors—Hugh Lake, John Christiansen, Chuck Green, Bob Cargo, and Jeff Jakes. Special thanks to Robert Wolgemuth, Pat's dear friend and literary agent since the beginning of his writing career.

David would like to especially thank Mark Bates, Jerry Bridges, Dr. Rod Cooper, Tim Keller, Richard Lovelace, Jack Miller, John Piper, Paul Tripp, and Tedd Tripp. And thanks to Ruthie for helping make the words come to life.

We both would like to thank the faithful staff of Man in the Mirror for bearing with us: Pam Adkins, Zuleida Aleman, Jim Angelakos, Carlene Bone, Dick Bradley, Ken Brashear, Kim Cawby, Bernie Clark, Bill Clemmer, Brett Clemmer, Corrie Cochran, Doug Cottrell, Tracy Dickerhoff, Jessica Christopher, Betty Feiler, Tom Hingle and the night crew, Daphne Hinkley, Jason Hoag, Cheri Hulke, Jessica Lane, Marge MacDonald, Kirby McFallin, Kevin McMillan, Kelly O'Byrne, Dennis Puleo, Mario Rodriguez, Tracey Searles, David Simard, Andrew Templeton, David Tindall, Brian Tinker, and Mary Triller. The distinguished anthropologist Margaret

Mead once said, "Never doubt the power of a small group to change the world. That's about the only way it has ever happened." You are that group.

We deeply appreciate the literary refinements—not to mention their belief in us—of John Sloan, Dirk Buursma, Lyn Cryderman, John Topliff, Greg Stielstra, and Scott Bolinder.

Introduction

If you're like most men, your time is precious. We won't waste it here. We'd like to introduce this book by making a few simple promises:

- This book won't become a long list of things to do and not do.
- This book won't bury you under an avalanche of guilt.
- This book will thrill your heart because you will see the "big picture" of fathering as you've never seen it before.
- This book will give you the practical suggestions you've been looking for to address the practical problems every dad faces.

Think of a man whose children grew up to cause him grief. Now think of a man whose children grew up to bring him joy. This is what is at stake here. "The father of godly children has cause for joy. What a pleasure it is to have wise children" (Proverbs 23:24 NLT). We feel honored to have a chance to share these thoughts with you.

A special thought for fathers of teenagers ... One dad put it well: "Being the father of teenagers has brought out the worst in me." From fourteen to twenty-two can be tough. We suggest that if your teenagers become rebellious, be careful not to do anything to make it impossible for them to return to you. Avoid anything that would permanently injure your relationship. We sincerely believe if you absorb and apply the following lessons about "fathering the heart," they will, in time, come back to you.

And if you don't read another page of this book, please tell each child every day "I love you," and "I'm proud of you."

CHAPTER 1

Why Another Book on Fathering?

"Why another book on fathering?"

That was the question that immediately came to mind when we decided to write this book. And it deserves an answer.

The short answer is this: This book will show you how to move from "fathering for performance" to "fathering the heart." But what do we mean by "fathering the heart"? And why is it so important?

FATHERING THE HEART MEANS NOT FATHERING FOR PERFORMANCE

Even the dullest observer, taking only a cursory look at the statistics, can see that the state of the family is getting worse, not better. So what's the problem? Is it because children are tearing their families apart? Sometimes, but it's the exception. Is it because mothers are abandoning their children? Every now and then you hear a sensational story like this, but only rarely. Who, then, is most responsible for this crisis? Could it be that fathers are not equipped to hold their families together?

We think it's about the dads.

Don't get us wrong. Most dads want to do the right thing—they just don't know what it is or how to go about doing it. So they do the best they can to control behavior, keep peace, urge better grades, keep "Mom" happy, and get through it. In short, they "father for performance." Because most of us know only the "fathering for performance" model, untold numbers of dads (who really want to do the right thing) are instead alienating yet another generation of kids. They pass on the sins of their fathers, repeating rather than breaking the cycle.

This book will show you how to build a gospel-based parenting *system* to "father the hearts" of your children. So what's our answer to the question? We *do* need another book on fathering, a book about fathering the hearts of your children to help you break the cycle of fathering for performance.

FATHERING THE HEART MEANS BREAKING THE CYCLE

We have a second, more personal, reason for writing this book. When a dad who grew up in a dysfunctional home breaks with the past, he sets an entire family on a new course for many generations. Does this sound like an overstatement?

Actually, we both know from experience the power of a dad who breaks the cycle and fathers the heart. We know, because both of our fathers broke the cycle for us, for our children, and for our children's children.

Pat's Story

When my dad, Bob, was just two years old, his father abandoned the family. To make ends meet, my dad's oldest brother, Harry, went to work on a bread truck before school, at the butcher shop after school, and at the filling station on weekends—at the age of ten.

When my dad turned six, he, too, went to work, helping out on the bread truck and delivering papers. The brothers got up at 3:00 A.M. every day and had a permanent tardy slip for school.

My dad's mother, Mae, suffered a stroke. The family soon lost its small farm and moved into town to live with two of Mae's sisters. Together these women reared my dad and his three siblings. And they did a great job! God gave these women grace, and God himself became my dad's dad. God said he would be "a father to the fatherless" (Psalm 68:5).

Pat's father, Bob Morley, is the little boy on the left. His dad had recently abandoned the family.

My dad never knew the warmth of a father's embrace, never felt the scratch of his dad's whiskers, never overheard his dad whistling or singing while he worked, never smelled his work clothes, never heard him joke around or read a bedtime story, never heard him say "I love you, son" or "I'm proud of you, son," never received a father's approval or guidance, and had to guess at what it meant to be a father to me.

Dad's Legacy

Bob Morley with Pat

My dad passed away last year. Dad never wanted his legacy counted in money or achievements. He had one mission in life: to break the cycle. By his determination and sacrifice, my dad was determined to give my three brothers and me what he missed.

I have many fond memories. My dad loved me. My dad invested in my life. He gave

Pat with his son, John

me his time. He attended my games. He took me to work with him. We shared chores on the five acres where we lived. My dad taught me what it meant to be a man—how to live with integrity, how to practice a strong work ethic, and how to treat a woman. I am what I am today because my dad refused to follow in his father's footsteps.

Like every man who misses out on having a good father, my dad had to decide if he would repeat the sins of his father or break the cycle. By God's grace, my dad chose to become a real man. My dad became the man he was in spite of his father, while I am who I am largely because of my father.

As I've considered Dad's life and the odds against him, I have, by God's grace, come to understand something important. While you measure the success and legacy of some men by how far they go, you grasp the secret to my dad's success and legacy only by seeing how far he came.

But all was not perfect in paradise. The problem was that Dad didn't know what a "normal" father looked like. He knew what he *didn't* want to be like, but he had no mental image of what he did want to be like. So he had to, in the words of dysfunctional family systems expert Janet Woititz, "guess at what normal behavior is."[1]

My dad and mom became religious. They wanted to bring us up in the church. They were looking for help in raising "normal" kids. Regrettably, while our church had many fine qualities, they had no vision or strategy to help my dad become a godly man, husband, and father. So part of this story is sad. My dad wanted to break the cycle, but instead, at the age of forty, after serving in all possible leadership positions in the church, he pulled our family out of church. I was in the tenth grade at the time. It threw our family into a twenty-five-year downward spiral from which it is only now recovering.

It's interesting. Dad wanted to break the cycle. It should have taken twenty-five years. By God's grace, my dad did build enough into my life that I was able to break the cycle for my children. But it took fifty years, not twenty-five. Our family went through—I went through—twenty-five additional years of pain and misery because no one taught my dad that which, ironically, he wanted to know. What kind of pain? I started out my adult life as an angry young man. My brother Robert died of a drug overdose at the age of thirty-one. My other brothers, though now doing well, have struggled with many difficult challenges. I can't help but wonder, *What if my dad had been part of a church that discipled him to be a godly man, husband, and father? How might our lives have been different?* I will never know. But you can.

My son, John, recently married. He and I were talking one day about the kind of career he wants to pursue. "Dad," he said, "you were always there for all my games. That really meant a lot to me. That's what I want to be able to do for my kids. I need a career that lets me do that."

It's true—I *was* there. I was there for him because, even though my dad didn't know exactly what to do, my dad was there for me. Because my dad broke the cycle and was there for me—even if imperfectly, I could offer my son and daughter an entirely new legacy. Whether your fathering experience more closely resembles mine, my dad's, or my dad's dad, in this book David and I will share some lessons to help you father the hearts of your children.

David's Story

My father, Bill Delk, is my hero. No man I know has started out with so little and ended with so much.

Dad grew up in a poor family in rural South Carolina. His father, a true renaissance man, succeeded at almost any task: repairing machinery, woodworking, farming, the trucking business, the pulpwood/logging business, selling and buying produce, sewing (he served in the Marines as a tailor), and working as a prison guard. He taught my dad many practical skills, including how to rebuild a tractor engine. He loved his family and generously helped those in need. Everyone in the community wanted to be his friend.

Just one problem: Those things were true only when he stayed sober, and my grandfather never stayed sober for more than six months at a time. Dad felt ashamed when his friends made fun of his father. He saw money wasted on alcohol that could have been used for clothes or food. Dad's family never had a television, telephone, or even an indoor bathroom. Worst of all, my dad lived in constant fear of what his father might do next to embarrass the family.

My grandfather's alcoholism forced responsibility on my father at a very young age. He became a surrogate father for his younger sisters. He also kept the business running—handling the bank account, getting equipment repaired, helping his mother talk merchants into selling groceries on credit, and paying enough to creditors to keep them from repossessing equipment.

At the age of fourteen, Dad helped my grandfather with the logging business. On many Saturdays, Granddad got too drunk to pay the workers or carry out his other responsibilities, so Dad had to handle everything for him. He drove to the pulpwood buyer to collect the week's money. Then he went to the bank, deposited the check, and withdrew cash. He calculated the workers' wages, deducted what they had borrowed against their wages, and paid them in cash on Saturday afternoon. My grandfather stayed in the pickup the whole time, either asleep or embarrassing my dad with his behavior.

Wilbur Delk, David's grandfather

My grandmother didn't go to church when Granddad got drunk, for fear that he would come looking for her. But Dad had an aunt who took him to church. Through this church he came to faith in Christ and vowed that, with the Lord's help, he would live a life very different from his father.

Bill Delk, David's father

After graduating from high school, Dad went to Georgia Tech, equipped only with a place to stay (at his aunt and uncle's), a co-op job, and $10 in his pocket. The $600 he made for his first three months of work was just enough to cover his first semester's tuition.

Bill Delk, David's son Ryan, and David

Early on he determined to give something better to his family. For him this meant providing materially and, even more important, providing spiritually. As a father, he made the investment to lay a spiritual foundation for his sons. I am who I am today because God graciously gave me a faithful dad who broke the cycle.

Whatever your own growing-up experience, whatever legacy you received from your own dad—good, bad, or none—there's hope. Pat and I honestly believe this book will fully equip you to help your own children love God and love others from their hearts. If you need to, you can break the cycle. You can leave a legacy that matters.

FATHERING THE HEART IS GOD'S PLAN

The family lies at the heart of God's plan. From the very beginning, God planned that, through the family, his message should be passed on to future generations (Deuteronomy 6; Psalm 78).

Picture yourself in church on Sunday morning. Let your mind wander around the congregation. Take a look at ten teenagers sitting near you. There's Jeff who works at the grocery store. Becky from down the street sits with her parents. Luis quietly talks to his girlfriend, Tammy.

With the faces of these young people still in your mind, consider this: *Eight* of these ten children likely will drop out of church by the end of their senior year in high school, and only *four* of them will return.[2] Why? What's going on? And what can we do about it? That's what this book is all about.

According to two Boston College professors, we have entered a period of the largest intergenerational transfer of wealth in history. They predict that an astonishing $40.6 trillion dollars will get passed down from parents to children during the years 1998 to 2052.[3] Yet at the same time, we are squandering a great spiritual heritage—so much so that, in many cases, very little spiritual wealth remains to transfer to the next generation. As we see more and more young people drift away from Christ and his church, one cannot help but wonder, *What will become of us? Will the church remain a viable force in the world in forty more years?* Dozens of other equally chilling questions demand answers.

The Bible shows us that this decline starts when a generation of dads fails to "deliver the goods" to the next generation. Judges 2:10 observes, "After that whole generation had been gathered to their fathers, another generation grew up, who knew neither the LORD nor what he had done for Israel." And what happened to them? The following verses show that this new generation "did evil," "forsook the LORD," "followed and worshiped various gods," and "provoked the LORD to anger."

And what did God do to them? Judges 2:14–15 tells us that the Lord "handed them over to raiders who plundered them. He sold them to their enemies all around, whom they were no longer able to resist" (at this point think alcohol, drugs, pornography, unwed mothers, sexually transmitted diseases, materialism, and so forth). God opposed them for a season, and they suffered greatly.

None of us dads, after even a moment's reflection, would knowingly "transfer" this kind of tragedy to our kids. Yet many of us received just this sort of legacy from our dads, and now we are repeating the cycle. That's why we suggest that unless God intervenes to turn the hearts of our fathers toward their children, we will lose this entire generation of kids.

Frederick Taylor, the father of Scientific Management, said, "Your system is perfectly designed to produce the results you are getting." Imagine yourself as a manufacturer of bicycles, and every third bicycle comes off your assembly line without a front tire. Your manufacturing system is perfectly designed to produce these flawed results. It works the same way in the family. Many Christian parents have a system perfectly designed to yield mediocre and even devastating results.

Even though most Christian dads would say their number one concern is making sure their children turn out well, many of these dads appear stuck on autopilot. They just hope and pray that somehow, some way, by the grace of God, their children will live for Christ. They love their kids, but they let them have too much say (any kindergarten teacher will name discipline as the number one problem).

More diligent dads often think they're supposed to get their children to do all the right things. They work hard at getting them to conform and to live up to a set of expectations. But they don't focus on their children's hearts. That's why so many "moral" children grow up to reject Christ. They say, "All Dad cared about was getting me to obey—but he didn't really care about me. Not personally."

We need a fathering "system" perfectly designed to disciple our children to love God and others from the heart.

FATHERING THE HEART MEANS ASKING "WHY IS MY CHILD DOING THIS?"

Like nearly all life-changing ideas, the central message of this book is simple. For too long, most fathers have fallen into one of two categories: those who neglect to love and train their children; or those who merely focus on trying to get their children to do the right things.

Both of these methods lead to dead ends. We know many men long for something more, because we hear from them all the time. We believe this "something more" can be found in what we call "fathering the heart." We desire to help men recover the spirit of Deuteronomy 6; Psalm 78; and Mark 12:29–31.

Our premise is that dads need to start by asking a different question—not "*What* is my child doing?" but "*Why* is my child doing this?" A father should focus *not* on getting his children to do the right things but rather to love God and others from the heart. When our children love God with all their heart, soul, mind, and strength, the right behavior will follow.

This book will both challenge and thrill you. While neither of us lean toward false bravado or showmanship, we believe in this message so strongly that we have a simple proposition for you: *We dare you to read this book and not be changed.*

LET'S MARCH!

In the fourth century B.C., Philip of Macedonia took control of several northern Greek cities. Down in Athens, the two greatest political orators of the day, Isocrates and Demosthenes, spoke out about the danger. Isocrates, a teacher, made sure he presented the facts well. Demosthenes, on the other hand, concerned himself not only with what was "true" but also with what could be "made true" by the actions he advocated.[4]

Both men addressed the threat that Philip presented. When Isocrates finished, people said, "How well he speaks!" But when Demosthenes spoke, they said, "Let's march against Philip!"

Men, we will give you the facts about fathering in this book— that we promise. But unless this book changes the course of your family for generations to come, we will not be satisfied.

Fathering the heart is the biblical method and the way of Jesus, and it is the method that could prompt the greatest revival in history. Because this book presents biblical truth in a way largely abandoned by generations of parents, we believe it has the potential to change the world, one family and one child at a time.[5]

Men, we need a parenting revolution. Parents must see that their mission is not merely to get their children to behave, but to believe. The Bible declares of Elijah, "He will turn the *hearts* of the fathers to their children" (Malachi 4:6, emphasis added). It's about the heart. We need parents who will fight for their children's hearts!

We believe this book contains the truth you've been searching for. So come, take this journey with us, and let's see where God leads. It's time to march!

We begin in the next chapter with an overview of what it means to father your child's heart.

THE HEART OF THE MATTER

- The family is getting worse, not better—and it's largely because of dads.
- Most dads want to do the right thing, but all they know is "fathering for performance."
- Both Pat's father and David's father broke the cycle, setting their families on a new course for generations to come.
- Only 60 percent of children reared in church remain in church as adults.
- Fathering the heart lies at the heart of God's plan.
- Fathering the heart means asking "Why is my child doing this?"

TAKE IT TO HEART
QUESTIONS FOR APPLICATION AND DISCUSSION

1. How does your story resemble Pat's or David's? How does it differ? What lessons can you learn from considering your own family's legacy?

2. Read Deuteronomy 6:4–9 and Psalm 78:1–8. How do these passages show that fathers have a crucial role in God's plan for the world?

3. Before beginning any spiritual exercise, it's a good idea to decide how willing you are to allow God to work in your life. What do you hope to gain by reading this book?

STRAIGHT TO THE HEART
Protecting Your Children from Shame

Do you remember that feeling of shame you felt as a child?

- Perhaps your father said something to hurt you: "You've been nothing but trouble ever since you were born," or, "You are so lazy and good for nothing!"
- Maybe a sibling said, "Get out of here—you aren't good enough to play with us!"
- Maybe a friend told everyone a secret that you thought would stay just between you and him.

Most of us can vividly remember times when others shamed us. Often it was just another bump in the road that we had to overcome. But sometimes these bumps devastated us. One forty-five-year-old man said, "No matter what I did, I could never please my father."

What makes shame such a powerful force? It strikes at the very core of our identity and dignity as people made in the image of God. Shame poisons the heart. Shame tells a child the lie that she must care for herself and that no one loves her for who she is. We cannot father the heart and shame our children at the same time.

Consider three important ideas to help you avoid shaming your children.

Watch What You Say

"I can't believe you could do something so stupid." "Why don't you try thinking for once?" "That's the dumbest thing I've ever heard in my life."

Perhaps you can still see and hear your father as he said such things to you. Maybe you've said this, or something like it, to your children. When we talk like this, our children feel attacked and humiliated. They hear the derision and disgust in our voice. What do you think this does to the heart of a child? It's like taking a blowtorch to a wax candle—it melts the soul.

Treat Your Children with Respect

We need to treat our kids with respect. Too often we treat our children differently than we treat others. We talk to them in a tone of voice we would never think of using with anyone else. We ignore them when they speak to us or give them only a portion of our attention while we keep one eye on the football game. When we make our children feel like an interruption or an inconvenience, we create shame in their hearts.

Avoid Unrealistic Expectations

Children feel shame when we expect them to reason or perform at a level above their abilities. When four-year-old Brian opened the refrigerator door and knocked down his little brother, he really had no idea his brother had walked up behind him. Eleven-year-old Steve didn't consider that taking an hour longer to finish his chores meant he'd miss the big football game on TV. And fifteen-year-old Tammy never gave it a thought that failing to finish her project on Thursday night meant she probably couldn't be at a family picnic on Saturday.

We may want our children to think like adults, but they can't. Certainly we should discipline them for unacceptable attitudes and behavior, but we must not belittle them or expect them to think like adults. To father the heart, we need to have appropriate expectations for our children and gently help them grow in their ability to reason.

Fathering the heart means allowing your children to be children. It means celebrating who God has made them to be *right now,* rather than belittling them because they aren't yet what they will become. When children feel grace and acceptance from their father, their hearts grow strong with a love for God and others.

CHAPTER 2

What Is Fathering the Heart?

In order to know what something *is*, sometimes you have to know what *it's not*.

WRONG: FATHERING FOR PERFORMANCE

"My son is getting straight A's," boasted John's dad. "He's a starter on the football team, and, best of all, he isn't into earrings, tattoos, and all that weirdness. He's not like so many kids today."

Too many Christian dads concern themselves primarily with how their children perform. As long as their children perform well—doing okay in school, looking clean-cut, saying "please" and "thank you"—these fathers believe everything's fine. Yet the Bible says, "Man looks at the outward appearance, but the LORD looks at the heart" (1 Samuel 16:7).

When we father for performance, our discipline becomes a way to get our children to stop doing something we don't want them to do. We establish rules and punishments to get our children to conform and to perform up to our expectations.

Fathering for performance means to focus on getting rid of unwanted behavior and replacing it with acceptable behavior. It may work for a while, but it stinks as a long-term solution.

Six-year-old Collin wouldn't stop punching his older sister. "Collin," his dad warned, "if you punch your sister one more time, you're going to be restricted to your room for twenty-four hours—

no TV, no music, just reading. Do you understand me?" Collin loved TV and music, so he resolved not to hit his sister. And he didn't— for two days. But when she irritated him again, he let his fist fly.

What's wrong with this picture?

Rebecca was getting unsatisfactory grades in school. "Rebecca," her dad said, "if you get all A's and B's on your next report card, I'll buy you that CD player you've been wanting." Guess what? Rebecca got all A's and B's. Her dad, with a sense of self-congratulation, happily took Rebecca shopping for a new CD player. The next term, though, she came home with two C's and a D.

What's wrong with this picture?

With enough *promise of reward* or *threat of punishment*, most children can exercise the self-control they need to perform for a restricted period of time. The greater the promise or threat, the longer the child can hold out. But a deeper problem exists. Despite how cute and cuddly he seems, left to his own nature (the flesh), Collin is not a nice, pleasant, self-controlled child. Despite the effort Rebecca put into getting good grades, it didn't come from the heart; she just wanted the reward. In these two examples, neither child became "different" because of their behavior. Their fathers attempted to control their behavior, but neither helped their children deal with the attitudes and beliefs of their hearts.

As a dad, you can get your children to behave for a while if you make a big enough promise or offer a big enough threat. Sooner or later, though, their true natures will come through. Eventually, they will reject this performance approach and begin to act out of what's really in their hearts—and usually at the worst possible time. That's why we have to grasp this difference between *performance* and *heart*. Their identity has to be molded by Christ to love God and others from the heart.

RIGHT: FATHERING THE HEART

By contrast, when we father the heart, we seek to go beyond *what* our children do to *why* they do it. Rewards and punishment have a place, but only when they are focused on changing the core affections of a child's heart.

One day, when the Morley children were young, Pat's wife was talking to a friend. This woman wondered what she could do to make sure her children never messed around with drugs. Patsy said, "For me, I'm not primarily concerned with their behavior. I'm interested first in what's going on with their heart." And that's the difference between fathering for performance and fathering the heart. Fathering for performance gets children to behave right. Fathering the heart helps children believe right.

In this book we want to help you understand the distinctions between these two fathering styles. We want to help you move from *fathering for performance* to *fathering the heart*. The following table gives you an overview of these two systems:[6]

Fathering for Performance	Fathering the Heart
Emphasis on conformity	Emphasis on transformation
Atmosphere of fear	Atmosphere of safety
Parental control	Freedom within boundaries
Focus on present performance	Focus on future development
Playing a role	Being authentic
Coming down on our children	Coming alongside our children
Surface interaction	True communication
Assumes the worst	Believes the best
Status quo	Growth and change
Pronouncements from on high	Questions and discussion
Uses people, "business relationship"	Intimacy and vulnerability

For the rest of this book we will develop the differences between these two fathering styles. We want to help you become a dad who fathers the hearts of your children.

FATHERING THE HEART MEANS SEEING THE BIG PICTURE

When David was a little boy, his dad, Bill, wanted to make sure his three city-raised boys knew how to do some "real work." So he took them back to the old family farm for a taste of what he had experienced as a boy—planting seedling pine trees by hand.

Pine tree seedlings have to be planted in the bitter cold of winter so they take root before spring growth and summer heat. Bill's boys didn't know what to expect. They felt even more uncertain when they arrived at the briar-and-bush-infested field their dad had selected. Looking over forty acres of grass and weeds, David and his brothers knew they weren't in the suburbs anymore.

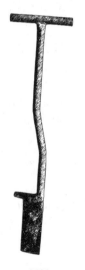

dibble

You plant pine seedlings with a strange-looking tool called a dibble. You slam the small wedge at the end of a waist-high handle into the ground, push the wedge forward and backward to create a hole, plop the seedling in the hole, pull up the tree a little to straighten the taproot, push the dibble forward to seal the deal, and finally stomp a couple of times for good measure. Then it's pick up your five-gallon seedling bucket and do it again. For nine-year-old David, it seemed like a never-ending job.

But you have to be careful—plant the seedlings too close, and they'll grow up tall and skinny. So Bill taught his boys how to count off the right number of paces between seedlings, then mark the spot for the next tree.

The boys found it difficult to walk in a perfectly straight line, because the thick snarl of briars and underbrush seemed to reach out and grab at their feet. How could they keep their rows straight?

Bill solved the problem by using a trick he learned as a boy. He cut down some small trees and made them into poles, then lined up two poles at the end of each row, one behind the other and about ten feet apart. "Boys," he instructed, "after you count off your steps, lift your eyes. If those two poles at the end of the row line up, then you'll know you're in the right spot."

Our world today has a lot in common with that field—a tangle of briars and brush that make it difficult to find, much less stand in, the right spot. Temptations and pressures grab at our feet all day long. We dads need two poles on which we can fix our eyes to make sure we're lined up properly with God's plan.

David's dad understood something his boys didn't. You can't complete the task without looking at the big picture. You won't find the right spot unless you remain in line with the goal. He passed on a powerful lesson to the next generation. You can too.

FATHERING THE HEART MEANS PURSUING THE RIGHT GOAL

What would you say is the goal of a father? Take a moment to form an answer before reading the rest of the chapter.

If you asked a random sampling of men on the street, "What do you see as the goal of a father?" you would get many answers and, no doubt, more than a few blank stares. Some would say, "It's to teach our children to be responsible adults." Others might say, "To help our children get educated for life." Still others would say, "To help our children find happiness and success." Many on auto-pilot wouldn't even have an answer because they've never stopped to consider their goal as a father.

If you asked men in your church, you would hear a few additional answers. Some would say, "The goal of a father? It's to get our children to obey Christ." Others would talk about their children growing up to become productive members of society and the church. But very few would get to the heart of the matter.

While we could restate the biblical goal of a father in any number of ways, in this book we will state it simply: *The goal of a father is to disciple the heart of his child to love God and others.*

FATHERING THE HEART MEANS DISCIPLING YOUR CHILDREN TO LOVE GOD AND OTHERS

When someone asked Jesus to name the greatest command-ment, he replied that all the Law and the Prophets could be summed up in one statement: "Love the Lord your God with all your heart and with all your soul and with all your mind and with all your strength. . . . Love your neighbor as yourself" (Mark 12:30–31).

God created us to enter into a relationship of love and worship with him. He made us to bring him honor and glory. He created us to depend on him for everything. Have you ever found anything that could satisfy your heart except Christ?

What "best thing," then, can we do for our children? We can lift our eyes and focus on the goal of a father. We can help our kids "line up the poles" so they can grow up loving God and others. We can do nothing greater for our children than to help them change the core affections of their hearts.

This is the essence of the gospel. Our culture lures us—and our children—to focus on our own needs and happiness. Even the church can get overly focused on what God does for us. But the gospel tells us that we find ourselves when we lose ourselves in loving God. The message of Christ is not a self-help message about how we can change our lives for the better. Instead, he tells us to renounce our self-reliance and desire for independence from God and instead trust him with our whole hearts. As Pat's pastor says, "It's not about us."

Christ doesn't give us a rulebook and tell us to make sure we follow the rules; he gives us a new heart and a new desire to glorify him. So does this make obedience and behavior unimportant? Hardly. But they do come in second. Behavior flows out of belief.

Christianity is not about behavior modification; it's about heart trans-formation.

When our children receive Christ they become "new creations" with transformed hearts. As they grow in Christ, they find a new desire to love and obey him.

This is what it means to father the heart. This is what we must teach our children. Only this will get them out of the briar patch. And this is the goal of a father.

FATHERING THE HEART MEANS DRIVING OUT FOLLY

A young man named Cameron said, "All summer long I made one dumb decision after another. I got myself in a lot of trouble." Cameron believed that his summer escapades of drinking, late-night parties, and egging the neighborhood would make him happy. They didn't.

Adam's fall into sin in the Garden of Eden made it certain that all children will naturally attempt to make it on their own without God. If they don't believe that God will take care of them, they will try to take care of themselves.

And what keeps our children from loving God and loving others from the heart? What's the main counterforce to living a godly life? The Bible calls it "folly." Proverbs 22:15 reads, "Folly is bound up in the heart of a child, but the rod of discipline will drive it far from him." We dads have to solve the problem that the hearts of our children are "bound up" in folly. That's why we must father the heart.

Every dad wants wise children. And a dad who wants to father the heart of his children must start by dealing with his children's folly.

What is folly? The dictionary calls folly a "lack of good sense or normal prudence and foresight."[7] Good sense and prudence for what? Spiritually, folly is to believe that something other than God can bring meaning, satisfaction, or happiness. Folly believes the lie that "Christ alone is not enough to make me happy. I need something else." Folly amounts to idolatry because it loves something more than God.

Because sinful men and women like us created our culture, it perfectly appeals to the folly living in the sinful part of our hearts—

and our children's. Our culture's emphasis on physical beauty, for example, tempts many children to believe that their appearance will bring them happiness. Some kids want to perform better than others so they can become successful and gain respect. Others pursue pleasure through their senses in order to feel happy. Some children expect money and material things to make life easy and bring them joy. Still others experiment with drugs, alcohol, pornography, or sex to escape their problems and find peace.

Why is it so crucial to deal with the folly bound up in the heart of a child? Because children grow up and take their hearts with them. Notice what Proverbs 19:3 observes: "A man's own folly ruins his life, yet his heart rages against the LORD."

You've heard the saying, "There's no fool like an old fool." It's true. But how does a fool get to be an old fool? Obviously, he starts as a young fool, whose father fails to help him overcome his folly—who doesn't help him line up the poles.

Dads, the writer of Proverbs tells us that folly is the greatest problem we face. Every child enters this world with folly in his heart, and if it goes unchecked, this folly will grow until it ruins his or her life. We know. It ruined the life of Pat's grandfather. It ruined the life of David's grandfather.

Positively, our goal as fathers is to disciple the hearts of our children to love God and love others. We have to set up these two poles as life markers. Negatively, our goal ought to be to rid our children's hearts of folly, to clear out the briars and underbrush that keep them from standing in the right spot.

Dad, remember that folly is bound up in the *heart* of a child, not in his or her *behavior*. Their behavior merely expresses what's going on in their hearts—their *beliefs*. Foolish behavior flows out of foolish belief. The Bible puts it this way: "Out of the overflow of the heart the mouth speaks" (Matthew 12:34). The only way to deal with folly is to go beyond external performance and to father the heart.

Christian parenting—the kind we propose in this book—goes way beyond just "what" our children do (their behavior). We want to teach you how to question and mold "why" they do it (what's going on inside their hearts; see 1 Kings 1:6).

We want to act as God's "dibbles" to plant our children in the soil of Scripture so they can take root in Christ and grow to full wisdom. Put a child in the right spot, clear the brush, and line up the poles, and God will transform our children from the inside out.

Before we can understand the "why" of our children's hearts, we must understand the big picture about what happens to the hearts of children as they grow up in a sinful world, and how the message of Jesus provides the antidote for their folly. In the next chapter we'll take a look at "Understanding Your Child's Heart." After that, each chapter will explore a different practical way you can disciple your children to love God and others "from the heart."

THE HEART OF THE MATTER

- The goal of a father is to disciple the heart of his child to love God and others.
- Christianity is not about behavior modification; it's about heart transformation.
- Man looks at the outward appearance, but God looks at the heart.
- Behavior flows out of belief.
- The heart of a child is bound up in folly—the belief that something other than God can bring meaning and happiness.
- Fathering the heart involves driving out folly.

TAKE IT TO HEART
QUESTIONS FOR APPLICATION AND DISCUSSION

1. Review the chart (page 31) that compares "Fathering for Performance" with "Fathering the Heart." Which method best reflects your childhood, and why? Which method best reflects your fathering system to date, and why?

2. Suppose we had just met on the street, and we asked, "What would you say is the goal of a father?" Describe the answer you would have given before you read this chapter. What new thoughts, if any, has this chapter given you about the goal of a dad?

3. What is folly? Why is it so important to help our children overcome their folly? Give an example of how one of your own children has recently displayed folly.

4. "Christianity is not about behavior modification; it's about heart transformation." What does this mean, and what does it imply for your role as a dad?

STRAIGHT TO THE HEART
Dealing with the Pressures Dads Face

Today's dads catch it from all sides. "Briars and weeds" poke at our legs all day long. It's tough to keep our eyes on our main goal of fathering the heart.

How are you handling the pressures you face? On a scale of 1 (No Problem) to 5 (Completely Swamped), rank how each of the following pressure areas affects you:

_____ *Career Pressure*—Many of us have the same commitment to our jobs as workers did thirty years ago, yet we have become much more aware of the importance of our commitment to our families. So we try to work hard to advance in our career while also attending Boy Scout meetings, Valentine dances, and Little League games.

_____ *Temptation Pressure*—Most men see more than a thousand logos and advertisements each day, all of which insist their product has the key to happiness. Sexual images are splashed on everything from billboards to newspapers. Scores of catalogs entice us to buy things we don't need to please people we don't like. No matter what we have, we always lack that one more thing.

_____ *Technological Pressure*—If you had bought a house thirty years ago, the last round of negotiations to finalize a contract might have taken several weeks, since everything had to be done by mail. Today, three or four rounds of changes can take place in several hours through the use of faxes, e-mail messages, and the Internet. Most men face technological pressure every day from voice mail, cell phones, beepers, and e-mail. Some businessmen are expected to respond to five hundred or more e-mail messages a week.

_____ *Money Pressure*—Compared to the standards of a hundred years ago or to current Third-World countries, almost every working American is wealthy. With these riches comes the ability to make choices. We decide where we want to live, what kind of car to drive, the type of furniture we will own, the leisure activities we will enjoy, which of forty-seven types of cereal we will eat, where we'll go for vacation, and on and on. Ironically, more choice brings not only more freedom but more pressure.

_____ *Relational Pressure*—Most of us live in a neighborhood with one set of people, work with another set, play sports or engage in hobbies with others, and go to church with yet another group. With today's fragmented lifestyles, it's not easy to develop and maintain lasting and meaningful relationships (or to keep up with everyone if you try).

What pressures do you face? What has God already done for you that could free you up? If you feel overwhelmed by your pressures, we encourage you to get involved with other men who can help sort things out—begin or join a small group. Go to http://www.maninthemirror.org for some resources to help you get started.

CHAPTER 3

Understanding
Your Child's Heart

Eight-year-old Kelly didn't feel well when she went to bed. As she crawled under the covers, a pain shot through her stomach. When her father came in to say good-night prayers, she told him, "Daddy, my tummy hurts real bad."

Her mom and dad figured it had to be something she ate, so Mom headed to the medicine cabinet and came back with a tablespoon of Pepto-Bismol. Finally Kelly got to sleep.

A few hours later, a sharp bolt of pain awakened Kelly. She grabbed her stomach, curled up in a fetal position, and started sobbing. Her mother heard her cries and came to investigate, with Dad not far behind. They quickly realized something serious was happening. They put some clothes on Kelly, woke her brother and dressed him, then rushed to the emergency room.

"Please, help us. We don't know what's wrong." The ER nurses and doctors sprang into action, and soon one of the doctors announced, "I'm afraid she has appendicitis." Kelly's parents signed the papers authorizing surgery, then anxiously sat down in the waiting area. An unusually busy night in the ER forced them to wait through the rest of the night, the morning, and well into the next day. By the time orderlies finally wheeled Kelly into surgery, her appendix already had ruptured. Though that complicated the surgery, everything went well, and today Kelly is doing just fine.

What a powerful lesson for fathering! Even when we sincerely believe we are helping our children, we can totally miss the mark. When we father for performance, we think we're administering the right medicine, but we completely misdiagnose the problem. Why? Because we don't understand their hearts. When we father for performance (behavior) and neglect fathering the heart (belief), it's as though we give Pepto-Bismol for a ruptured appendix.

FATHERING THE HEART MEANS DEALING WITH EACH CHILD'S "DUAL IDENTITY"

Trent's algebra teacher wrote, "Trent is the kindest young man in class. He treats his fellow students with respect." His startled dad read the teacher's comments, then turned the report card over to make sure it was describing *his* Trent. Shaking his head, he put down his reading glasses and wondered, *What does she know that I don't know?*

Are our children good or bad? They're both, of course. All of us have a "dual identity." We reflect God's image but are products of the Fall.

Images of God

The Bible teaches that our children are made in the image of God—think of them as little "images of God." Every child has innate value, dignity, and worth by virtue of his or her creation in God's likeness. God knit us together in our mothers' wombs (Psalm 139:13) and made us a little lower than the angels (Psalm 8:5). Our children truly represent God's greatest achievement, the full expression of his creative genius! This is a child's true heart.

Little Sinners

The Bible also sees children as "little sinners." Any father of a two-year-old knows that his child has a good acquaintance with the Fall! Every child has a sinful nature by virtue of having sinful parents. The apostle Paul wrote, "There is no one righteous, not even one; there is no one who understands, no one who seeks God" (Romans 3:10–11). This sinful nature gives our children a distorted view of themselves, God, and the world. This is a child's "false" heart.

As Pat has written elsewhere, "The paradox of man is that he is a product of both the Creation and the Fall. The Creation made him like a god, and the Fall made him like a devil."[8] As dads who father the heart, we must help each of our children accept their dual identity. Once they face their sin, Jesus can re-create the image of God in them through repentance and faith.

FATHERING THE HEART MEANS HELPING YOUR CHILDREN DISCOVER THEIR TRUE HEART

Because children instinctively recognize themselves as creatures of dignity, they often behave in ways designed to gain acceptance and feel worthwhile.

Brian's father repeatedly told him, "You're worthless. You'll never amount to anything." Something inside of Brian cried out, "No, that's not true! I am not worthless!" His instincts rebelled against his father's insults.

By the time Brian entered middle school he had become the class clown, always laughing and pulling practical jokes. He found acceptance by making people laugh. Deep down in his heart, of course, he felt only as worthwhile as his last practical joke. He felt rejected by the one person who really could have made him feel accepted.

All children feel compelled to determine who they are, to discover their identity. Children have a desperate need to know that they are okay, that they are acceptable. You may not speak to your children as Brian's dad did, but they still need you to validate their worth. We can best help our children find their "true heart" by walking with them down the path of life, helping them understand how to find their identity in Christ, not in their performance.

Children don't transfer their source of identity to Christ overnight. Many adults who know Christ still struggle every day with this issue. During the years that our children work this out, the world has a powerful impact on their hearts.

We can't help our kids unless we understand them. What does our culture do to a child's heart? What shapes their hearts? How can we recognize the chief patterns? Consider four categories (discussed in the next section) that can help you zero in on the state of your children's hearts. Look for the dominant tendency—that's the heart you want to father! Consider how you might protect your child's heart from spiraling into a wrong pattern.

FATHERING THE HEART MEANS HEALING DAMAGED HEARTS

A child's heart may have become a . . .	What is this heart looking for? What does it love?	What does the gospel offer? How does Christ meet the real needs of this heart?
Bruised Heart *Seen in:* insecurity, lack of initiative, depression	Approval Validation Attention Support	*The gospel says:* It's okay if life disappoints me, because God will take care of me. (Hebrews 13:5)
Inflated Heart *Seen in:* talking too much, insensitivity, selfishness, demeaning, arrogance	Happiness Power Admiration Possessions	*The gospel says:* It's okay that I'm not perfect, because God sees me as perfect in Christ. (Romans 3:21–22)
Hard Heart *Seen in:* distant, loner, self-protecting, cold, mean	Protection Truth Justification Approval	*The gospel says:* It's okay to allow myself to feel, because in the end God will not let me down. (1 Corinthians 1:8–9)
Addicted Heart *Seen in:* hunger, fixation, desperation, drivenness	Pleasure Escape Coping Possessions	*The gospel says:* It's okay to desire pleasure, but you'll find lasting pleasure only in God. (Romans 15:13; 1 Peter 1:8)

Let's explore each of these four hurting hearts in more detail.

1. A Bruised Heart

Tommy had struggled with his weight for as long as he could remember. His parents had a hard time convincing him—at eleven years old and 175 pounds—that he would enjoy playing Little League baseball. Tommy finally decided to play and actually began to have more and more fun as the season wore on. Because he was slow, the coaches put him at first base. His soft hands and good coordination allowed him to become a solid contributor to the team.

He had a much harder time as a batter. He had trouble swinging with much force while maintaining his balance. But Tommy was determined. He worked at it, and by the end of the season he could at least make contact.

His team's last game of the season took place during the league tournament. Tommy came up to bat in the last inning, his team trailing by one run with no one on base. He swung at the second pitch and hit a line drive over the pitcher's head into center field. He lumbered to first base and barely beat the throw from an alert center fielder. Tommy felt ecstatic—he'd just gotten a hit in the most important game of his life!

He heard the coach yelling his name from the dugout. He couldn't help but smile as he turned to hear some expected words of congratulations. Instead, he saw his coach motioning for him to return to the bench. As he slowly left the base, he saw a teammate running out to take his place. Then the reality set in—he'd been yanked for a pinch runner. As he entered the dugout, the pats on the back from his teammates felt more like ridicule than congratulations. Tommy made his way to the corner, sat on the bench, then buried his head in his hands and silently sobbed.

All of our children will feel like Tommy at some point in their lives. We cannot protect them from the suffering that makes up an inevitable part of life in a fallen world. What happens to a child's heart when life seems to slap him down again and again? Sometimes his heart gets bruised or crushed.

A child with a bruised heart feels beaten down by life. She believes she can never be good enough to live up to the expectations of those around her. He feels ashamed, fearful, and insecure, and often decides it hurts too much to try and so fears to take a chance or to risk losing.

Such children become tentative and self-protective, believing that if they don't look out for themselves, then nobody else will. They withdraw and don't give themselves to anything out of fear of getting hurt. They seem overly sensitive and can easily become emotional. They often begin a downward spiral of despair and hopelessness difficult to overcome.

Jesus Christ has an answer for a bruised heart. He is "gentle and humble in heart" (Matthew 11:29), and the prophet said of him, "A bruised reed he will not break, and a smoldering wick he will not snuff out" (Matthew 12:20). Jesus wants bruised or crushed children to remember that "it's okay if life disappoints me, because God will take care of me." Many of the following chapters will give you practical ideas to bring this message to a bruised heart.

2. An Inflated Heart

Angela always had a gift for music. At thirteen, she played the piano better than many students about to graduate from high school. She enhanced her natural gifts by her dedication to practicing an hour every day. Angela had some tough times at home with her mom and dad, but when she sat down at the piano, everything seemed okay. She practiced all year for the district competition, and both she and her teacher felt confident she would take the top spot and move on to the state level.

At the competition, Angela listened to the other students perform and rightly judged herself the best pianist of the group. When her turn came, she played a Mozart sonata flawlessly and with incredible emotion. When the judges announced the winner, they called Angela's name. As Angela walked to the podium to accept the top prize, she felt glad the judges recognized how well she had played. She bowed to her fellow students and to the audience before walking back to her seat.

Some children protect themselves by trying to be the best in an effort to avoid failure or disappointment. This child believes that her self-worth comes from how well she performs—and she expects to perform well. Children like this become proud and often act in condescending ways toward those who can't perform at their level. They seek approval from an "inner circle" of peers who validate their performance and help them feel okay.

Ironically, an inflated heart often develops as a response to lingering feelings of inadequacy and self-doubt. Because a child feels deep inside that he doesn't measure up, he gravitates to an area where he can excel. Then he invests so much of his identity into his performance in this area that he cannot admit any weaknesses or deficiencies. One of the best ways to keep up this facade is to constantly criticize and identify the weaknesses of others.

Jesus helps inflated hearts by giving us complete acceptance that is not based on performance. God loves us, not because of what we do, but because of the "righteousness from God [that] comes through faith in Jesus Christ to all who believe" (Romans 3:22). God enables the inflated heart to say, "It's okay that I'm not perfect, because God sees me as perfect in Christ."

3. A Hard Heart

"Jeff, I'm home!" From his room, Jeff could clearly hear his father's voice, but he didn't respond.

"Jeff, where are you?" Jeff rolled over and turned the page in his comic book without saying a word. He heard his father's footsteps coming up the stairs. Then his dad appeared in his doorway. "Hey buddy, what are you doing?"

Jeff turned another page and continued to read.

"I'm sorry I missed the scout meeting tonight. I really wanted to be there. We had a meeting at work that ran long, and then I had to take care of a few things afterwards. Did you have fun?"

Jeff spoke without looking at his father. "It was alright."

"Well, I promise I won't miss next week. I've got it on my calendar."

"We don't have troop next week."

"Well, then I'll be there the week after that. How does that sound?"

"Sounds great, Dad," Jeff said with a small sigh. He hoped his father would leave so he could get back to his comic book. The X-Men had gotten into a really tough spot, and he wanted to finish it before bedtime.

Some children respond to the pain of life by becoming hardened. Such children feel tired of disappointment and hurt. They respond by shutting down emotionally and cutting themselves off from their heart. They often do not display "normal" emotional reactions to situations. They are afraid to feel, because they are afraid of the pain.

When they do allow themselves to feel, the depth of their anger often surprises them. They may lash out both verbally and physically. Emotions make them feel out of control, and so they try to stuff their feelings. It seems easier not to feel than to deal with a lack of control or the pain of disappointment.

A child with a hard heart needs to come to grips with the reality that, because of the Fall, disappointment will often invade our lives. But they also need to know that this world is not our home and that God has promised to bring us into an everlasting life of joy, peace, and fulfillment. Jesus wants a child with a hard heart to believe that "it's okay to allow myself to feel, because in the end God will not let me down."

4. An Addicted Heart

Alicia looked in the mirror and liked what she saw. Her new outfit really did look good. She knew her mom and dad didn't like to pay this much for clothes, but when they saw how she looked, they would realize it was worth it. She couldn't wait to hear what her friends had to say!

Everything went great until lunchtime, when Jennifer Thomas came into the cafeteria wearing a new outfit of her own—an ensemble clearly much more expensive than Alicia's. And if that weren't embarrassing enough, Jennifer looked better in her new outfit than Alicia did in hers.

As Jennifer approached the table where Alicia and her friends sat, Alicia stood up and gave her a quick hug. "I love your outfit. Is it new?" Jennifer answered and Alicia smiled, doing her best to hide the disappointment she felt inside.

Some children respond to the disappointments of life by latching on to people, places, or things that they believe might meet their deepest needs. They commit themselves to an activity, person, or possession way out of proportion to its true significance. They fixate on getting all A's in school, making the cheerleading squad, playing a video game, or wearing exactly the right clothes.

They always look for the next thing that may satisfy them. Met goals become a string of increasingly hollow victories that leave them wanting more. They feel driven to perform or experience. Their desires consume them. These things become an escape, a way to help them avoid dealing with the emptiness they feel deep in their hearts.

Naturally, our children want to escape from the pain of life. But the escape mechanisms that this world offers all lead to dead ends. Jesus wants our children to "store up . . . treasures in heaven, where moth and rust do not destroy" (Matthew 6:20). He wants them to believe that "it's okay to desire pleasure, but you'll find lasting pleasure only in God."

FATHERING THE HEART MEANS NOT
FALLING INTO THE PERFORMANCE TRAP

All of these hurting hearts develop because our children struggle with a sin common to all of us: We want to perform well so we can say we are good enough. We would love to be able to make it on our own without God's help. Then we could say, "God, look at what a good person I've become! Aren't you happy with me?" This is why fathering for performance causes so much damage—it feeds our children's belief that it is up to them to satisfy God.

Sin causes our children to feel that they must earn acceptance through good performance. They know they can't measure up to God's standards (or even to their parents' standards), so they believe they must choose one of two responses:

- They defend their own goodness. It's too painful to admit that they are unacceptable, so instead they become defensive and shift the blame to others. Sometimes they put on a face of false bravado and pretend they can handle it. They find it hard to "go down."
- They despair over their own sin. Because they believe their self-worth depends on how well they do, their mistakes and failures send them into a tailspin. They find it hard to "come up."

FATHERING THE HEART MEANS
HEART SURGERY, NOT PEPTO-BISMOL

Most of us, including our children, live our lives based on a poisonous formula (we were unable to identify the source of this formula):

$$\frac{Performance}{Expectations} = Acceptance$$

(Our performance divided by our expectations determines our acceptance)

We believe our acceptance is based on how well we perform, compared to the expectations we set for ourselves. Theresa always got A's in school, so she felt devastated when her report card showed a B for Spanish (Performance B ÷ Expectation A = Feelings of devastation). Eric had promised himself he wouldn't scream at his sister again, but now he found himself yelling at the top of his lungs. A few minutes later he felt terrible.

Even if we try to lower our expectations to make ourselves feel okay, at the core of our hearts we know we've failed to live up to God's standards. Derek didn't intend even to look at his report card—he didn't care what it said anyway. Still, he couldn't help taking a peek when he saw the open envelope on the kitchen table. Chrissy ran to her room to avoid another lecture from her father about coming home late. Still, as she cried into her pillow, she wondered why she couldn't get along with her dad.

For too long we Christian fathers have administered Pepto-Bismol when our kids needed heart surgery. We've tried to get our children to conform their behavior without dealing with the attitudes and beliefs of their hearts. Our fathering style has implicitly and explicitly led them to believe that their performance determines their acceptance.

Only one thing can break this cycle: helping our children experience God's grace and complete acceptance in Jesus Christ. At the core of their being they need to believe that God loves them, not for what they do or don't do, but because of what Jesus has done. They can freely accept the reality of both their dignity and their sin, because God accepts them in Christ. If our children grasp this, their renewed hearts will enable them to become everything God wants them to be.

Can you think of any more important need for the world today? Look around at young people, and you will quickly see a brutal reality: Many of them suffer not from a ruptured appendix but from something much more devastating—a shattered heart.

THE HEART OF THE MATTER

- Children have a dual identity: the dignity of creation in the image of God and a sinful nature from the Fall.
- Children have a desperate need to know they are okay.
- Fathering the heart means helping our kids find their identity in what Christ has done, not in their own performance.
- When the world shapes our children's hearts, they can become bruised, inflated, hard, or addicted.
- When judging themselves by their performance, children will either defend themselves or despair over their failures.
- We break this cycle by helping our children experience complete acceptance in Jesus.

TAKE IT TO HEART
QUESTIONS FOR APPLICATION AND DISCUSSION

1. What significant events shaped your heart as a child? Which of the four types of hearts best describes you as a child?

2. Which of these hearts best describes each of your children? What steps can you take to address the state of each child's heart?

3. Do you truly believe that your performance has nothing to do with your acceptance? If so, how did this come to be? Identify some ideas that can help your children come to this same conclusion.

STRAIGHT TO THE HEART

Healing the Father Wound and the Mother Wound

As dads, we are all influenced by our own childhoods. Just recognizing the forces that have shaped us can begin a process of healing and renewal.

Pat has recently gone through professional Christian counseling. Even though he had a solid, caring family, he did not feel deeply loved as a child. His parents didn't tell him they were proud of him, and they showed little interest in him as an adult. Their behavior probably reflected only a lack of training on their part, but it had the same negative effect, whether intended or not. Take some time to reflect on a few important questions:

- Do you feel that your dad truly loves you, and why?
- Do you feel that you are special to your dad—that he takes delight in you—and why?
- Do you feel that your dad is proud of you, and why?
- What kind of emotional connection do you have with your dad?
- Do you feel that your mom loves you, and why?
- Do you feel that your mom has an unconditional positive regard for you—that you are the "gleam in your mother's eye"—and why?
- Do you feel that your mom is proud of you, and why?
- What kind of emotional connection do you have with your mom?
- Did you feel well prepared to be a father? Why or why not?

Almost all men can see how their father's impact plays out in their own behavior. Some men see this as a blessing, as they observe positive values passed on to the next generation. For others, this feels painful, for they see the hurt and shame of their own past repeated in their own efforts as a father.

No matter how good your father was, his faults still left an imprint on you. And even if your father was never around, his absence left an indelible impression on your heart. This "Father Imprint" affects how we father our own children.

Less obvious, and less discussed, is the impact our mothers have on our general sense of well-being. If we did not feel properly loved—if we didn't feel "precious" to our mothers— even as adults, we still feel like little boys with a hole in our hearts.

How can we go beyond these "imprints" to become everything God wants us to be? Consider a few practical steps you can take:

Express your feelings to your dad or mom. Meet face-to-face with him or her or write a letter. If your dad or mom is deceased, consider writing your feelings in your own journal. Be sure to include your gratitude for the good as well as your hurt over the bad.

Confess your faults. No one is perfect. Just as our parents affected us, our reaction to our fathers and mothers influenced them.

Forgive your father or mother, if necessary. Forgive, but don't condone any negative behavior. Don't deny the pain either. Face it head-on, admit what you have lost, mourn and grieve over what you missed, and then move on. Don't wallow in the pain. Instead, let the Holy Spirit nurture you in the areas your dad or mom missed.

Commit to the relationship. Start over where you are. As one man says, "It's not important how it starts; what really matters is how it ends."

CHAPTER 4

Affirming
Your Child's Heart

Like many parents of small children, Pat and Patsy Morley tried to learn from other moms and dads. They attended classes at church and often sought counsel from friends. One weekend they had an opportunity to attend a parenting seminar presented by Larry Crabb. Twenty years later, Pat still remembers one important idea from the seminar—this Larry Crabb declaration: "Our children need to know, 'Yes, I love you, and no, you can't have your own way.'"

This is a huge idea. *Yes, I love you, and no, you can't have your own way.* Sadly, for many children growing up today, this message has gotten lost.

This statement captures the essence of the idea of affirmation. Remember how we said children are both "images of God" and "little sinners"? When we say, "Yes, I love you, and no, you can't have your own way," we speak directly to the core of this dual identity. We affirm our kids' need for grace and redemption. Fathering this way gives children security and creates an atmosphere where God can work in their hearts to help them love him and love others.

Affirmation has two parts: the expression of *unconditional love* and the idea of *structure*.

FATHERING THE HEART MEANS GIVING UNCONDITIONAL LOVE

Pat's brother Robert died tragically from a drug overdose at the age of thirty-one. After Vietnam, this troubled soul despaired of all the wickedness and evil that he saw men do to each other. He put his faith in Christ but never recovered a normal life.

Pat's mom and dad—for that matter, the whole family—loved Robert deeply, with no strings attached. They accepted him unconditionally. In the decade after Robert returned from Vietnam, the family did everything it could to help Robert help himself—methadone clinics, counseling, encouragement, and love—a lot of love. Whenever Robert did something that made you want to pull your hair out by the roots, Pat's mom would say, "It's always hardest to love the ones who need it the most."

Pat believes these cords of unconditional love gave his broken brother the desire to embrace Jesus as his Savior before he died. Robert is right now in the presence of Jesus because of unconditional love. Our children can endure almost anything when they feel that kind of love.

An affirming father makes sure his children feel his unconditional love. No force in the world has more power. When our actions and words say "I love you," it affirms our child's heart. They hear "I am worthwhile. I have dignity." It also can help them grasp the love God has for them in Jesus Christ.

Let's face it. In most situations our children will be judged by their performance. If they stink at kickball, they will get picked last for the team. If they don't get high enough grades, they can't take advanced classes or join the honor society. If they get labeled as not pretty enough or not cool enough, the "in crowd" will refuse to accept them.

All of these situations tell our kids that their performance determines their acceptance. "You're only as good as your last game [or report card]." Children can easily come to believe that they must always do something more to win the acceptance of others. They ache to be "good enough" in the eyes of those around them.

It's Dad to the rescue! Dad can give his kids the unconditional acceptance and approval that the rest of the world makes conditional. Who better than a dad to counter the message, "You are valuable only if you can perform"? Our kids need to *believe*, deep in the core of their being, that they are loved and accepted no matter what they do. Then they will enjoy the security of love, despite their status as "little sinners."

Christ's gospel insists that God does not love our children because of what they have or have not done; he loves them because of what Christ has done. Many children (and dads!) find this idea difficult to grasp. Unconditional love creates an atmosphere where they connect with this truth, because they've already seen it in an affirming dad.

FATHERING THE HEART MEANS PROVIDING STRUCTURE

When David was growing up, his parents made it clear that they didn't do life the same way many other families did. For example, David was not allowed to see many of the movies and TV shows that his friends watched. He also couldn't stay out as late as other kids or go to some of the parties they attended. At first, David felt as though he was missing out. But as he grew older, he trusted his parents more and thought less about what he might be missing. Now David feels grateful that his parents provided structure to help keep him on the right track.

When we say to our children, "No, you can't have your own way," we give them structure. Structure gives our children security. The boundaries we establish say to them, "You don't have to face life's tough decisions on your own." A lot of children today grow up so fast that their hearts can't handle it.

Our kids face tremendous temptations. Sex, materialism, gluttony, anorexia, bulimia, drugs, laziness, addiction to video games— our children are constantly bombarded with the opportunity to seek something other than God to meet their deepest needs.

Compared to a hundred years ago, children also have to make more decisions on their own at increasingly younger ages. Children in day care make small decisions each day without the input of their parents. Latchkey children decide what to do, what to watch, or where to go. Fifty-nine percent of children nowadays come home to an empty house.[9] Research shows that most teen sex takes place in homes after school when both parents are working outside the home. And in many places "bigger sinners" offer sex and drugs to "little sinners" in their preteen years.

Every home needs structure. A problem Pat has endured for the last couple of years provides a perfect illustration. Pat's driveway connects two roads. The only way to move between these two roads—other than by using his driveway—adds about a half-mile to the trip, so kids regularly cut through his driveway.

Pat usually works at his home office, and the frequent use of his driveway shortcut has driven Pat absolutely loony. His two dogs bark every time a kid rides his bike through the property. And the dogs don't just bark; they go crazy. Once they start, they shut up only when someone stops what he or she is doing and gives the dogs a treat.

For a long time Pat didn't know what to do about this annoying problem. The situation came into focus a few months ago when the house of a neighbor several houses away caught fire. Pat had never met this neighbor, so he hurried down the street to see how he could help. After introductions, the man said to Pat, "I really appreciate you coming down, and, by the way, where do you live?" Pat tried for some time—without success—to explain the location of his house. Finally the guy said, "Oh, I know. You live in the cut-through house!"

Pat promptly said good-bye and sulked all the way home. He even had to walk home in the rain, which seemed appropriate. When he got home, he said to Patsy, "That's it! I'm not going to be known as the guy who owns the cut-through house. I've got to do something about this!" When he outlined his first idea for protecting the sanctity of his driveway, Patsy had to explain why a chain across the driveway that would catch a kid on a bike about chest high wouldn't look good for a Christian author.

Instead, Pat decided to buy a sign. He visited several hardware stores but found nothing except big signs that said KEEP OUT or NO TRESPASSING. In order to be a good neighbor, he thought he should soften the message a little, so he made his own sign, which read, "THIS IS A PRIVATE DRIVE. I WOULD APPRECIATE IT IF YOU WOULD NOT USE THIS DRIVEWAY AS A CUT-THROUGH. THANK YOU! OWNER." He put up his sign at the end of the driveway.

It made absolutely no difference.

A side road runs beside Pat's house, and one day Pat heard two kids on bicycles while he sat in his backyard. He ran around the house in the other direction and, sure enough, caught the two kids cutting through the driveway.

"Hey, you two kids," Pat called out. "We need to talk. What are you doing? Can't you see that sign out there? This is a private driveway."

Pat felt terrible when one of the two children started crying. "Jason," said the older boy to his younger brother, "you don't need to cry."

"That's right, Jason, you don't need to cry," Pat reassured. "We'll get this worked out."

After Jason calmed down a little, Pat said to both brothers, "You do understand that this is a private driveway, right? You know enough to realize that this does not look like a public road. This is made of concrete and it's lined with flowers and bushes. It's next to a house. This is not a main road. You understand that, right?"

"Well, yeah, we saw the sign, but my father says we have to be home by 5:00, and the only way we can get home by 5:00 is to cut through your driveway."

"Whoa, whoa, whoa, wait just a minute!" Pat replied. "First of all, it's not my problem what time you get home, and second of all,

all you have to do is drive up to the next road, which would take all of two extra minutes."

The kids left after saying, "Okay."

But Pat's dogs kept barking every day. About a week later, Pat caught the same two kids cutting through his driveway again. Do you know what the older brother said to him?

"I talked to my mother about it and she said that my father insists that we be home by 5:00 and it's okay for us to ride through your yard, and if you have any questions about it, you can call my mother. She said you could call her."

"Whoa, wrong answer, wrong answer," Pat replied. Even as he prepared to speak he thought that someone who would treat their children like this was exactly the kind of person who would sue a homeowner if their child had an accident on the property.

"Look," Pat said, "you are not coming through this driveway anymore. If your mom or your dad wants to talk to me about it, you have them come and see me and we'll talk about this. But I am not going to negotiate with an eleven-year-old."

You have to wonder, *What kind of father would put his child in such a situation?* This boy had no structure or support to help him act wisely. A father needs to actively provide guidance and not leave his child to make his own way.

We must provide structure for our children. Even if they put on a brave face, somewhere deep inside their hearts they realize that they cannot handle life on their own. Unless we give our children structure, they will remain afraid. Why? Because they know that they are in over their heads. Like Jason, they may bravely cut through your yard, but always on the verge of bursting into tears.

Kids who don't get both unconditional love and structure end up with an affirmation deficit. Let's look at the four fathering paradigms that come from different arrangements of "love" and "have your own way."

FATHERING THE HEART MEANS
NOT BEING A DISCONNECTED FATHER

"No, I don't love you, and yes, you can have your own way."

Thirteen-year-old Tim came into the living room to ask his dad if he could go to a violent, sex-saturated, R-rated movie with a friend and his father. His dad continued reading the paper and answered without even turning his head. "I don't care. If you want to, go ahead. Tell your mom what time you'll be home."

The disconnected father doesn't care enough to provide love and structure for his children. You may have had a father like this. His words may echo in your mind to this day: "I don't care what you do." What message lies behind these words? *No, I don't love you, and yes, you can have your own way.* Kids who grow up this way feel like "practical orphans."

A dad can also send this message by his actions, not just by his words. Divorce creates many absent dads. Twenty-four million of America's seventy-two million children under age eighteen—one in three—will go to bed tonight in a home without their biological father. Many of these dads want to be there—you may be one of them—but the research shows that most remain absent. After three years, most divorced dads have disconnected from their children (worth remembering as you think about the single moms in your church).

Other dads choose a career path that makes it impossible for them to stay around much. Their connection to their work leads to a disconnection from their children. They don't have much input into their children's decisions. Most of these fathers don't know what their kids do with their time. Most dads have trouble giving the names of their children's teachers, doctors, and the classes they're taking. A disconnected dad probably can't name even one!

Even though disconnected fathers may tell their children they love them during the rare times they do spend together, their children hear a different message: *No, I don't love you, and yes, you can have your own way.* A perpetually absent father has orphaned his children just as surely as the man who says, "I don't care what you do." He communicates, "'No, I don't love you,' because I'm not around, and 'No, I don't care what you do,' because I'm not showing any interest in what you do."

This sounds harsh, but it's true. Millions of children grow up in homes with disconnected fathers. Was this your experience? Then the lot now falls to you to break the cycle. You can do this!

FATHERING THE HEART MEANS NOT BEING AN AUTHORITARIAN FATHER

"No, I don't love you, and no, you can't have your own way."

Imagine that Tim lived in a different family. He walks into the living room and asks his dad if he can see the R-rated movie. His father explodes in anger: "You must be kidding me! Why in the world do you think I would let you go to a movie like that? What kind of family do you think this is? Is that the way I raised you? There is no way I would ever let you see a movie like that!"

What message does his response convey? He may as well have said it out loud: *No, I don't love you, and no, you can't have your own way.*

The authoritarian father tries to control all aspects of his children's lives. He turns his house into a prison camp. This atmosphere inevitably creates shame in the heart of a child, because such children know they cannot live up to their father's expectations.

Sometimes children catch this message even from an absent father. An overly strict father who travels too much or works late every night says the same thing to his children. They know that he doesn't consider them a high priority. They may not hear the words, but the message comes through loud and clear: *No, I don't love you, and no, you can't have your own way.*

FATHERING THE HEART MEANS
NOT BEING A PERMISSIVE FATHER

"Yes, I love you, and yes, you can have your own way."

Suppose that when Tim asked about going to the R-rated movie, his father put his arm around him and said, "Sure, son, whatever you want to do."

The permissive father tries to be more of a friend than a parent. A lot of fathers think that, in order to parent successfully, they have to become their kid's best friend. That's not what our kids want. In high school Pat's kids told him, "Dad, we don't want you to be our best friend. We want you to be our dad."

It feels very tempting to compromise what we believe so that our kids will like us, doesn't it? To let them go to the movie, stay out past curfew, ride in cars with older kids, play before doing homework, and so on. In fact, most of us are pulled in this direction. But if we allow our children to do things we believe are wrong in order to show that we love them, we say to them, *"Yes, I love you, and yes, you can have your own way."*

We shouldn't try to buy the love of our children by always letting them have their own way. Instead, find legitimate ways to show your children you love them so you can say no when you need to say no.

FATHERING THE HEART MEANS BEING AN AFFIRMING FATHER

"Yes, I love you, and no, you can't have your own way."

Suppose Tim comes into the living room and says, "Dad, can I go to an R-rated movie with Spencer and his dad? All my friends say it's not that bad."

His father puts down the newspaper and asks, "Tim, do you know what the movie is about?"

As Tim explains, his father asks him if he thinks it's appropriate for a young man of thirteen. They talk it over and agree that the movie isn't appropriate for Tim to see at this time.

Our children need the affirmation of knowing they have both *unconditional love* and *structure.* The affirming father helps his children see both sides of this reality. Affirmation helps a child understand his or her dignity as a person created in the image of God. Children who feel loved grow up to believe that they are special, created for a great calling and an important destiny.

Structure provides affirmation because children want and need boundaries. The world is a scary place, and they need to know they don't have to face life alone. When we provide structure for our children, we relieve the pressure of making choices and facing situations for which they are not yet ready.

God himself uses structure to redirect our hearts toward him. At its essence sin amounts to wanting to get our own way. Since the fall of Adam, we're all tempted to believe that if we just get what we want, we will find happiness. Ironically, often we get angry with God for not giving us things that would destroy us if we received them.

FATHERING THE HEART MEANS SAYING BOTH "I LOVE YOU" AND "YOU CAN'T HAVE YOUR OWN WAY"

When you father the heart rather than fathering for performance, both "I love you" and "you can't have your own way" share the spotlight. An unconditional "I love you" from an earthly father gives his children a sneak preview of the unconditional love and acceptance of their heavenly Father. A firm "you can't have your own way" prepares them for the security and happiness they find only through obedience to Jesus Christ.

Clearly sending these two messages to our children will help shape their attitudes and beliefs. They put big-time deposits into a child's emotional bank account. Your children will feel affirmed. And affirmation helps you accomplish the goal of a father: to disciple your children to love God and others from the heart.

THE HEART OF THE MATTER

- Our children need to hear "yes, I love you" and "no, you can't have your own way."
- Affirmation includes both unconditional love and structure.
- Unconditional love helps our children experience the grace of God.
- Structure gives children the security of knowing they don't have to handle life on their own.
- If we don't give our children both love and structure, we can become a disconnected, authoritarian, or permissive father.
- The affirming father shapes the heart of his child with both love and structure.

TAKE IT TO HEART
QUESTIONS FOR APPLICATION AND DISCUSSION

1. Which kind of father did you have: disconnected, authoritarian, permissive, or affirming? How has your father influenced your own fathering?

2. How does the Bible guide you to be an affirming father in Matthew 17:5; Ephesians 6:4; and 1 Thessalonians 2:11–12?

3. Rate how well you've done in striking a proper balance between unconditional love and structure.

4. What issue do you currently face with your children, and how can you affirm your child with "yes, I love you, and no, you can't have your own way"?

STRAIGHT TO THE HEART
Dealing with Grief

David's wife, Ruthie, went out on a recent Friday night and left David home with the children. After David had finished putting the kids to bed, he began to secure the house. Before locking the back door, he opened it to let Gracie, their black cocker spaniel, out of the house one last time.

Like many dogs, Gracie had learned the routine and often beat David to the back door. On this night, however, she didn't come when David opened the door to let her out. David shut the door and moved quietly through the house, looking to see if she might be hiding somewhere. When he couldn't find her, David went outside and called her name. Still no sign of Gracie.

Gracie had never run away before. When Ruthie returned home, she and David took turns driving around the neighborhood, calling Gracie's name. They kept this up until 1:30 A.M. On Saturday morning, they broke the news to the children that Gracie had vanished. The family made signs and put them up at stores and on light poles within a few miles of their house. They called their neighbors and friends to let them know what had happened and asked them to be on the lookout. They called friends at church and asked them to pray.

Gracie's collar displayed her name and phone number, so when Saturday night and Sunday morning passed without a word, David began to believe that perhaps Gracie wouldn't be coming back.

Sunday morning church felt brutal. David sat by his nine-year-old daughter as she began to sob during the first hymn.

David began to weep with her—nothing feels more painful than seeing a child with a broken heart.

After church, the family's lunchtime routine took on a somber tone. David took the opportunity to share several truths with his family:

It's okay to be sad. Losing a well-loved pet shows that we live in a fallen world. One day God promises that he will remake the world into the new heavens and the new earth, and everything will be exactly as it should be. Feeling sadness now should make us long for the day when God makes everything right (see Romans 8:18–27).

God knows what it's like to be sad. He watched his own Son die on the cross. Not only that, but he turned his face away and poured out his wrath on Jesus so that you and I could find salvation from our sin. We may not know why God allows sad things to happen, but we know that if he can turn Jesus' death into something good, then he can redeem our suffering as well (see Romans 8:28–39).

Children will experience loss in a variety of ways—the loss of a pet, the death of a loved one, or moving away from friends. Walk through these situations with your children and remind them of the reality of God's abiding love.

Fortunately for David's family, this story has a happy ending. Late Tuesday evening, more than four days after Gracie disappeared, they got a phone call reporting that she had been found. She had wandered more than three miles from the house, across a highway and a six-lane road! Once Gracie returned home, the house was filled with three happy children, one happy dog, and a very happy mom and dad.

CHAPTER 5

Roots and Wings

It really is tougher to be a kid today than ever before.

A cover story in *USA Today* explained how a phenomenon called "freak dancing" overwhelmed schools at the beginning of the new millennium. The article began, "At [a dance club], a handful of kids meld into a kind of Conga line that redefines the term 'joined at the hip,' as boys thrust their pelvises into girl's behinds to the throbbing bass of a hip-hop anthem.... One halter-topped girl stoops so far over the floor that she looks like a center trying to snap a football—except she's also gyrating wildly against the boy's groin."

We are just quoting the article—don't shoot us!

One young person says it's just the way everybody dances. "Honor roll kids do it," the article says. "Church-going kids do it."

"The difference now," educators say, "is that the moves are becoming more sexually explicit. Kids straddling each other, sandwiching one another."

One sixteen-year old girl says, "We don't get raunchy. It's not like we're getting naked." She says she has her limits, like "when guys put their hands down her pants." "I have morals," she insists. "I walk away."[10]

It makes us wonder, *What could happen to a girl's heart that would cause her to think that way?* Actually, it's quite simple. Folly is bound up in the heart of a child. She must not have a dad willing to guide her heart into wisdom.

Never has there been a tougher time to be a kid—but never has there been a time with more opportunity to make a real difference in the lives of your children. In this chapter we will offer an almost fail-safe method to father your children's hearts and prevent this kind of tragedy from happening to them.

FATHERING THE HEART MEANS MENTORING

Pat recently heard a report that made him feel very good. Many years ago he raced motorcycles. He dreamed of one day earning a factory ride—being sponsored by one of the manufacturing companies. (Instead he writes books and works with men—oh, well!) Not long ago a friend pulled him aside and told him, "I thought you'd like to know that my son's shop teacher said, 'The fastest guy I ever saw on a motorcycle was a guy named Pat Morley.'" Whoever that teacher is, Pat's nominating him for Teacher of the Year!

Pat's parents came to watch him race only once. Pat felt excited they had finally planned to see one of his motocross races. Because of limited funds, Pat always repaired his motorcycle himself.

On this day, after a big jump the handlebars gave way. Pat lost control and crashed on the landing area. Since Pat knew this was a blind spot for the other riders, he quickly jumped up to get out of the way. At the same time he turned around to see the action. Just then a rider sailed over the jump, his front tire hitting Pat square in the middle of his helmet, knocking him to the ground.

Pat wanted to make sure his parents knew he was all right, so he leaped to his feet and started waving. Then he looked down, saw blood gushing out of his arm, and passed out. The next thing he remembered, he was in a helicopter on his way to the hospital. His parents never came to another race.

By contrast, one of Pat's competitors came to every race with his dad. They had a van, a little tent, and all the right equipment. This father taught his son all the things he needed to know, giving this young man a real advantage. This boy had someone to mentor him and to show him the way. Pat remembers wishing he had a dad like that.

But how could he? Pat had pushed his parents away. Like many teenagers, he'd often said to his dad, "Leave me alone. I don't want you around." As a high schooler, after his family had dropped out of church, Pat hadn't allowed his dad to get involved in his life.

As a result, Pat became a very angry young man. You couldn't always see this anger from the outside. He looked happy, smiled a lot, and joked around. But just below the surface a silent rage simmered, ready to erupt at the slightest provocation. He ended up with quite a chip on his shoulder.

Pat often says, "The problem was that I had too much say." Many teenagers have the same problem—perhaps you were one of them. When a child pushes his parents away—and they let him do it—he ends up feeling as though he's on his own, that it's all up to him. He has to discover things on his own that other young men learn from dads who mentor them.

Hindsight is 20/15, a little better than 20/20. As adults, many of us look back and see the good qualities in our fathers that we overlooked as kids. And that's good. Still, it can't change the past. If you lacked a spiritual mentor, you had a huge deficit in your life. A mentor—a wise and faithful counselor—blesses a child in countless ways. Every child needs one, and without such a person, a child will grow exasperated and may end up disgracing his or her parents. All children need someone to help shape their hearts.

More than anything else, Pat regrets that his dad actually believed him when he said things like, "Leave me alone." Today, Pat wishes he could have said, "Dad, when I tell you I don't want you around, don't believe me. I'm lying. Those things are coming from a heart of folly. Don't believe me, Dad. It isn't true. I need you in my life every day." But as a foolish child, he did not have that kind of wisdom.

A foolish child knows what he wants but not what he needs. When our children try to push us away, we need to push back. A child may try to push you away, when the child really wants you to say, "Yes, I love you, and no, you can't have your own way." Anything less will exasperate our children. The apostle Paul writes, "Fathers, do not exasperate your children; instead, bring them up in the training and instruction of the Lord" (Ephesians 6:4).

FATHERING THE HEART MEANS BEING A DAILY DAD

Have ever tried to grow a vine? You start by planting the vine next to a structure such as a trellis. Then, as the plant grows, you discipline it. You train the plant to go where it's supposed to go. Sometimes you prune a branch; other times you simply wrap a branch around a part of the structure. If you don't do this on a regular basis, the vine becomes wild and grows every which way.

Like vines, our children need daily interaction and attention. They need us to remain present in their lives in tangible ways. Proverbs 29:15 reads, "The rod of correction imparts wisdom, but a child left to himself disgraces his mother." A child left on his own will disgrace his mother—he will become wild and unruly. A child without involved parents soon heads for trouble. Our kids need a daily dad.

FATHERING THE HEART FOSTERS INDEPENDENCE

Imagine a young toddler venturing out from her father while knowing that, anytime she wants to, she can run back and cling to Daddy's leg. This is how our children best develop.

From the very earliest age, what does a child want to do? She wants to become independent. One of the goals of parenting is to help our children become independent from us but still depend on God.

The Bible instructs us, "A man will leave his father and mother" (Genesis 2:24). It is the natural order of things. A mother weans a child from her breast, beginning the process of training the child for independence. We feel excited when a baby first rolls over. We feel more excited when a baby who can roll over begins to crawl. We get even more excited as this baby takes her first steps. Why? Because we want the child to become independent from us while still depending on God.

When the child becomes an adolescent, friendships become very important. Why? Because the child wants to become independent. Then the child becomes a teenager, and, of course, the stereotype goes that everything breaks down at this point. Why? Because the child wants to be independent. "Give me the car keys, please." And what does Mom say? "I'm not ready for my baby to drive!"

Eventually you work this out. Your child climbs into the driver's seat while Mom or Dad sits in the passenger seat with white knuckles. "STOP! You're getting too close to that car! Put your blinker on!"

"Mom, Dad, give me a break here. Can't you see I'm trying to become independent?"

The child somehow survives and learns to drive by himself. Why? Because he wants to become independent. Then about the time the child reaches his senior year in high school, everybody goes crazy. Why? Because this child wants to be independent. "Please go to college, get a job in San Francisco." "You never listen to me, Dad. You need to let me be my own man."[11]

FATHERING THE HEART DOESN'T ENGAGE IN POWER STRUGGLES

Nearly all conflicts in child rearing result from power struggles over the process of becoming independent. Either a child wants too much independence or the parents want too much control. (Of course, sometimes the child doesn't want enough independence or the parents don't want enough control.)

Basically, all of childhood comes down to an endless variation on the same scene: the toddler ventures out while always feeling the security that she can run back to Daddy's leg. That's why two of the greatest gifts a father can give his child are roots and wings—the wings of independence and the security of roots.

Regrettably, statistics bear out that most children today are not getting roots and wings. They have to figure out on their own the things that other kids are doing with a lot of support. What are the results? Both children might succeed; in fact, both will likely succeed at some level—but it won't be the same. One will have a healthy heart with the confidence and security of a sound support system, while the other will have an angry heart that feels as though no one really cares.

Your child's bravery in becoming independent will grow in direct proportion to how much security he or she feels. We've all seen a little child wander away from her parents in a grocery store with a great, big smile. But when she turns around and can't find Mommy, what does she do? She bursts into tears. Why? Her security has evaporated.

Adults do the same thing; we just hide it better. We get ourselves into a mess, we feel as though we have no one to turn to, and we burst into tears. Oh, we don't do it in a grocery store aisle where people can see. Instead, we do it at 2:00 A.M., haunted by fear, confusion, or regret.

FATHERING THE HEART GIVES WINGS OF INDEPENDENCE

We provide security for our children when we give them wings of independence. Wings grow when we interact with our children about identity, purpose, calling, vision, mission, education, and vocation. A child needs her father to tell her things. If he doesn't tell her, she will probably learn them on her own—putting her at an extreme disadvantage.

Pat's son, for example, has worked with Apple computers for a long time. During his freshman year of college, he ran a "Why Macintosh?" website out of his dorm room. One day when Pat visited, he said, "John, what's that under your bed there?"

"It's a server."

"Server for what?" Pat asked.

With a sigh, John replied, "I put together this little website about the Mac, and now there are about twelve hundred people from all over the world on the site. They're in chat rooms, uploading articles and downloading articles."

"Wow," Pat said, "I'm glad I didn't unplug it."

When he became a junior, John applied to Apple Computer for a job as a campus representative. Based on a couple of outstanding letters, the regional representative of Apple interviewed him one Tuesday morning. The man said he would let John know his decision on Friday.

In your experience, how good are the chances the guy would actually call on Friday? No better than fifty-fifty, right? Things come up when you're hiring, and you have to work on your own agenda. You may have given a date, but you don't feel bound to calling the interviewee at the advertised time.

So at midday on Friday, when no call had come, Pat phoned John and said, "Son, just so you don't get your expectations up too high, there's a good chance you're not going to hear from this guy today. It would be a very normal business practice for him to delay to Monday."

Why did Pat say what he did? To mentor his son in the way the world works (and also because his wife kept asking every fifteen minutes if the man had called).

Did the man call on Friday? No. Did Pat's son worry about it all weekend long? Yes. But he didn't worry like he would have if his dad had not acted as a mentor and told him what to expect. He got the job on Monday.

What would an inexperienced youth do who had no mentor? He might have called the representative and spoiled the whole thing. Then what would have happened to his heart?

FATHERING THE HEART MEANS HELPING YOUR CHILDREN IDENTIFY THEIR GIFTS

You can help your children to find their wings by encouraging them to discover something they do well. Make this a concrete goal, so that by the time your children leave your care they will have identified all areas of natural ability, aptitude, and spiritual gifting.[12]

Why is this so important? Because this is likely how God will use your children to make a unique contribution. Give them the opportunity to try a variety of things until they find their strengths and motivated abilities. Of course, fathering the heart means being careful not to emphasize their performance so much that they find their identity in what they do.

Bruce constantly struggled with his weight as a child. He had few friends and didn't enjoy trying new things. At the age of eight he began to sing in a church choir. Before long he sang his first solo.

Bruce can still remember the smile on his dad's face after his performance—the first time he had ever felt acceptance and pride from his dad. So Bruce poured himself into music. To this day he wonders whether he has invested too much of his self-esteem and identity in his musical performance.

Help your children find something they do well, but don't put so much emphasis on it that your child thinks doing well is the key to your approval—or God's.

Let your boys be boys and pursue activities that require energy, aggressiveness, and strength. Let your girls be girls without artificial limitations. Take care to counter the negative messages against femininity and manhood in culture. For example, make sure your daughters grow up believing that being a wife and mother is a holy vocation. Make sure your boys grow up knowing both the strength and selflessness of biblical manhood.

FATHERING THE HEART GIVES ROOTS OF SECURITY

In order to love God and others, our children need more than wings of independence; they also need the security of roots. Solid roots involve a host of things: relationship, safety, security, protection, stability, predictability, encouragement, solace, comfort, unconditional love, acceptance, approval, being there with your kids, and remaining a reasonable person.

David became a great king, but he failed miserably as a father. Eli made a great priest, but he reared wicked sons. The prophet Samuel stood in the gap for God, but his sons failed to walk in his ways. Each of these great men of God was pierced with child pain. While we can take small comfort that even great men of God can have children who don't turn out well, our pain remains very real. The Bible says, "To have a fool for a son brings grief" and "A foolish son is his father's ruin" (Proverbs 17:21; 19:13).

We suspect that if you could interview the freak dancers from the *USA Today* article, these children would tell you one of two things:

- "My dad doesn't care about me at all," or
- "All my dad wants is to get me to live up to his rules and expectations."

What kind of people do you like to hang around? Do you like to spend time with incessantly negative people? Do you like to hang around somebody who always interrupts you? Do you enjoy the company of someone who never shows you respect but talks down to you all the time?

What kind of dad do you think your children like to hang around? They like to stick close to the same kind of people we like to be around. Dads, let's commit to be the kind of father our kids love to have around!

We think developing three "fathering the heart" habits, in particular, can give your children the security of strong roots.

The Habit of Encouraging

Positive relationships create security—and negative ones take it away. Consider Harry. He has a knock on everything, a critique for every news story. To his credit, he finally recognized it. "You know, I have six kids," he said, "and when I walk into the room, within ten minutes they are all gone. I am such a negative person."

What would your children say about you? Nurturing fathers have a positive attitude. They constantly encourage and build up their children's hearts. Some parents tell their children who they are now and all the things they need to change. We think a better way is to tell them who they can become and encourage them to get there.

Why not visualize what you could see each of your children becoming—a warrior for Christ, an outstanding student, a terrific husband or wife, a super mom or dad, a great entrepreneur, a fine friend, or whatever else? Then bless your sons and daughters by giving them a vision for what they can become.

The Habit of Listening

Listening means not interrupting your children to give advice about what they ought to do or not do. Most of us dads think of ourselves as pretty wise. When our children come to us with a question, we already know the answer. But when we don't listen, our child's heart withers a little more and she walks away discouraged.

Before Dan's son got married in 2002, he said to his mother, "You know, Mom, you've always been my number one fan." That took Dan by surprise, because he always thought he was a coequal number one fan with his wife. So why did Dan's son see only his mother as his number one fan? Because she had spent more time listening through the years.

The next time one of your children wants to talk, why not put everything down, focus completely on what he or she is saying, and listen deeply without giving a reply? In fact, if you have a reply, why not say instead, "You know, I would like to think about that. Can I talk to you again in, say, fifteen minutes?"

The Habit of Caring

Our children live in environments where people don't really care. They should know at least that their dads really care.

When Steve was away in the army and then at college, he knew he could call his mom and dad anytime he wanted to—but he also felt as though they would never call him. Looking back, he knows they thought they were just giving him space. But at the time, he felt as though they didn't really care. Your kids do need space, but even more, they need to know that you care. If you feel unsure about whether you are giving your children too much or too little, just ask them!

FATHERING THE HEART MEANS TO GIVE THE BLESSING

What happens to children who go without the benefit of strong roots and wide wings? They build their hearts into a fortress. Some of them end up like some boys Pat recently met. A chaplain invited Pat to speak to hard-core youth offenders, fourteen to seventeen years of age, at the county jail.

Pat asked the chaplain what offenses the boys had committed. "Basically," he replied, "they're in for murder, rape, weapons, armed robbery, but mostly drugs."

"And how many of these young men have a father figure in their life?" Pat asked.

"Maybe 10 percent," the man answered.

Pat prayed and wondered what he, a white, middle-aged businessman, could say to these young men. He knew he couldn't give them "the" blessing—the blessing that only a father can give—but he still wanted to give them "a" blessing.

When he arrived, he handed each boy a name tag and said, "I'll tell you what this is for in a few minutes."

About halfway into his message, Pat asked each of the boys to write his own name on the name tag and put it on. Then Pat dropped to one knee in front of the closest young man. He read the name tag, then looked into his eyes and said, "Carlos Riviera [name disguised], God knows your name, and he loves you very much. He knit you together in your mother's womb. He knows every word you speak before it leaves your tongue. He knows when you sit and when you rise. He knows your thoughts from afar. He knows everything you've ever done, and he wants to forgive you. If you will open yourself up to him, he will open himself up to you. God wants to adopt you and be your true Father. You can change your life. Do you understand this?" Carlos nodded. Pat heard a few snickers.

Then Pat moved on to the next boy and did the same thing. By the time he got to the fourth or fifth boy, he could have heard a pin drop.

When they broke up the meeting, Pat said, "You know, I'm a hugger. So if anybody needs a hug, come on up here, and I'll give you a hug."

Twelve young men immediately lined up to get a hug from Pat. Then they stepped out into the hallway, where the guards shackled them to another prisoner and marched them back to their cells.

How had they ended up there at all? These young men had not received the blessing of roots and wings. Contrast their experience with the story of Kevin and his dad, Brett.

FATHERING THE HEART MEANS ORCHESTRATING RITES OF PASSAGE

In three weeks Kevin would graduate from high school. Brett wanted to do something special, something that would initiate his son into manhood. All through high school Kevin had grown especially close to two Christian friends. Brett decided to include the dads of these others boys, and so they made their plans together.

Kevin's girlfriend called him to say that she and two friends had designed a special outing for Kevin and the two other guys. Kevin and his buddies got excited. They expected a fun night out. The day finally came, and Kevin and his friends picked up the girls.

Then the girls blindfolded the boys and drove them around for a while. Before long, Kevin had lost his bearings. At last the car stopped, and the girls helped the boys out. Then they led them down a path and across a footbridge. Kevin could hear the sounds of the forest, so he knew they must be in the woods.

The girls led Kevin and the other boys to chairs arranged around an old fire pit and told them to sit down. One of the girls said, "Don't take off your blindfolds until we tell you to."

Kevin heard the girls walk away and cross the bridge. He heard car doors slam, the engine start, and a car drive away. Then nothing. Nothing but a deathly silence.

Meanwhile, Brett and the fathers of the other two boys stood around the fire pit with a handful of other men who had invested in the boys over the years.

After a long few minutes, Brett told the boys in a deep voice, "Remove your blindfolds." Kevin took off his blindfold and could not believe it. He felt completely overwhelmed to see these men surrounding him in the woods. What happened to the girls? He sat in stunned silence with no idea of what was about to happen.

The men gave their boys three short torches lit from the fire. Brett, the other dads, and the other men gave spiritual advice to Kevin and his friends, then asked each of the boys to kneel down. Each man went to the boys and prayed a blessing on their lives. Then they extinguished the three short torches and lit three tall torches in their place. And that is how Kevin and his friends received their initiation into manhood.

Kevin's dad fathered his heart. What a different story from the boys in the county jail! When you effectively father the hearts of your children, you give them roots of security and wings of independence. It could make all the difference in the world.

THE HEART OF THE MATTER

- A mentor gives wise and faithful counsel to a child.
- Give your children wings of independence by mentoring them and helping them identify their gifts.
- Fathering the heart means being a daily dad.
- We want our children to become independent from us while still depending on God.
- Almost all conflicts in child rearing come from the tension of independence and control.
- Give your children the security of roots by encouraging them, listening to them, and caring for them.
- Father the heart by giving your child the blessing and orchestrating rites of passage.

TAKE IT TO HEART
QUESTIONS FOR APPLICATION AND DISCUSSION

1. Did your father or another adult mentor you? If so, how has the experience left a lasting impact on your life?

2. Define mentoring. Why is it so important to mentor our children?

3. Ephesians 6:4 instructs fathers not to make their children angry but to train and instruct them in ways approved by God. What does the passage imply if we don't train and instruct them? What does it imply if we do?

4. In this chapter we used the metaphor of a toddler venturing out, while always feeling it can run back and cling to the security of Daddy's leg. In what ways does this picture capture the lifelong task of a child and you, the child's father?

5. Do you think you have the right attitude toward your child's desire to be independent? Why or why not? What can you do to give each of your children the confidence to venture out and the security that you will always be there?

STRAIGHT TO THE HEART
Rites of Passage

Can you remember when you first thought, I'm a man now? Did it happen at your high school graduation? Your first part-time job? Your college graduation? Your first full-time job? Did it take place on your wedding day? When exactly does a boy become a man or a girl become a woman? Unless you grew up in a Jewish home, you probably can't name a clear-cut experience.

Many cultures still retain ceremonies and traditions that mark transition points between childhood and adulthood (like the Jewish Bar Mitzvah and Bat Mitzvah). Unfortunately, American culture does not have such rites of passage. Yet a rite of passage will help your children *understand that they are entering a new stage in life.* Children need to know that God wants them to mature and develop. Some things that used to be appropriate are no longer appropriate. New responsibilities and privileges are open to them because of the milestone they have reached.

A rite of passage will help your children *build memories that help solidify their heritage.* Childhood can easily become an endless string of school, sports, music, television, homework, and church. Our children need some memories that stand out and give them a sense of family and tradition. These things can help us break through the everyday "noise" and speak God's message of grace and love straight to their hearts.

A rite of passage will help your children *understand the depth of your love and respect for them.* Rites of passage typically take effort—effort that your child notices. Make as big a deal about your event as seems reasonable—or even just a little bit more. Have Grandpa fly in as a surprise, rent a limousine for the big date, create a "memories" video of childhood footage, or have a certificate printed and framed. In general, more effort creates more impact.

So what can you do? Consider a few ideas:

- Schedule a date night with your eleven-year-old daughter. Have your wife buy a new outfit for her especially for the occasion. Bring her flowers on your way home from work. After dinner, stop for dessert and tell her how proud you are of the woman she is becoming. Pick a woman in the Bible, and tell your daughter the story of how God worked in and through that woman's life. Present her with a necklace, stuffed animal collectible, or some other item to help her remember the evening.

- Take your son camping for his thirteenth birthday and help him memorize the names of his grandfathers and great-grandfathers on both sides of the family. Tell him stories to help him understand his family history. End the weekend with the genealogy of Jesus Christ and a summary of how God worked through Adam, Noah, Abraham, and others to bring salvation to the world. Have several men from your church join you around the campfire and read letters they have written to your son. Put those letters in a scrapbook.

- Design a family crest or shield with your twelve- to sixteen-year-old sons. Select pictures or symbols that have significance for your family. Include images that teach biblical truth about our relationship with Christ and his call on our lives. Have an unveiling at a special dinner at which you invite other men to speak about different aspects of biblical manhood.

- Give your fourteen-year-old daughter an antique key and explain that it symbolizes the key to her heart. Tell her that God has given you the responsibility as her father to take care of her heart until she meets the man God has for her. Let her know that you will keep the key in a safe place. When she has found the man she believes God wants her to marry, give her the key to give to him.

- Take your ninth grade son and some classmates through a study group of *The Young Man in the Mirror: A Rite of Passage into Manhood*. Have a cookout at the end of the study, present each young man with a certificate, then have each father or spiritual mentor tell his young charge why he loves him and why he feels proud of him. When Pat did this with six other dads and sons, it became a very emotional time—especially for the dads!

- Read *Raising a Modern-Day Knight* by Robert Lewis.[13] This book has excellent rites of passage ideas.

Whatever method you use, the important thing is to make this a priority. Creating rites of passage for your children takes time, energy, and effort—but these rites offer wonderful ways to father the heart.

CHAPTER 6

Snake Lessons
and Dove Lessons

Pat enjoys sitting on his patio. A few years ago he buried an old wooden boat beside the patio and planted flowers in it. This past summer a black snake took up residence in the boat. Every few days Pat saw the snake make an appearance.

One day he watched the snake slither through the plants, stalking a lizard. The snake lunged for the lizard, but the lizard dodged the first strike and raced across the patio—straight underneath Pat's chair. Not to be denied, the snake took off in hot pursuit, also heading straight for Pat. Once it reached the hard surface, however, the snake lost traction and slowed down. The lizard got away.

Pat sat with his feet up in the air, wondering what the snake would do next. He looked over the side of his chair and saw that the serpent had come to a stop next to him. Pat bundled up the magazine he was reading and bopped the snake on the head. It quickly slithered back into the boat.

God has established an order to nature, a food chain. The lizard eats the winged insect; the snake eats the lizard; the owl eats the snake. And if the snake gets out of line, the man bops the snake on the head.

Our culture also has a food chain, and our children will enter it soon enough. We have already learned the importance of giving our children wings of independence and roots of security. Because many people out there are ready to "eat" our young, we must also equip them to make wise decisions.

Fathering the Heart Means Equipping Your Children to Make Wise Decisions

Remember the mega-problem we must deal with: "Folly is bound up in the heart of a child." Folly—or wisdom—reveals itself in decisions. As Pat was writing *The Young Man in the Mirror*, a high school boy on his advisory board said, "You should just name the book *Decision Making* because that's what it's really all about." The others nodded in agreement. Everything boils down to making good decisions.

Sonya's friends planned to go out for dinner and a movie, but she hadn't finished her paper for English and it had a due date just two days away. She really wanted to join her friends and thought she might have enough time to finish the paper tomorrow, but she decided to stay home and work on it that night to be sure—a good decision, since the paper took about twice as long to write as she expected.

Casey and his buddies finished a video game and headed out to his car in the parking lot. There was a lot of laughter as the boys hopped in the car. Casey backed out of his spot, then pulled forward without putting on his seat belt. One of the boys yelled something just as Casey approached the exit. When Casey turned to see what happened, he slammed into a car entering the restaurant. Even though they had accelerated to less than twenty miles an hour, the impact threw Casey into the steering wheel, breaking his jaw.

That's the way life goes: a series of little decisions, some good and some bad. Our lives basically end up as the sum of our decisions.

Sometimes what appear to be little decisions have big consequences. That's one of the frustrating things about making decisions. Often we can't tell how significant the consequences may be until after we make the decision.

David's daughter got a guinea pig at the end of last year's school term. Every few days, she took the guinea pig's cage outside and cleaned it. Sometimes, she'd leave the guinea pig outside for a while so it could enjoy the sunshine and fresh air.

One day, she cleaned out the cage and left it outside, then went with her mother to the store. If you've ever visited Orlando, you know that storms can blow up very quickly. A few minutes after they left, a thunderstorm rolled through, bringing strong winds and drenching rain. David's daughter had accidentally left the cage (with the guinea pig in it) just under the edge of the roof where water pours off during rainstorms. The cage had a solid bottom, which quickly filled up with water. The poor guinea pig drowned! To make matters worse, David was at home working and didn't think about checking on the guinea pig. They held a memorial service with lots of tears.

David's daughter had left the guinea pig outside dozens of times without incident. This time, however, the decision not to bring it inside had a traumatic result.

Children face decisions about things a lot more important than pet guinea pigs. That's why good decision making is key to our children's success in the cultural food chain. They need to know how to follow God's call in a world that will devour them unless they become prepared. How do we equip them to make good decisions about dating, sex, drugs, alcohol, smoking, money, becoming independent, identity, purpose, relationships, friendships, family, integrity, values, and so on? How do we help them to make decisions that reflect a love for God and others?

FATHERING THE HEART MEANS EQUIPPING CHILDREN FOR THE WORLD

Just before Jesus sent out his twelve disciples into the cultural food chain for the first time, he gave them some last-minute instructions. "I am sending you out like sheep among wolves," he said. "Therefore be as shrewd as snakes and as innocent as doves" (Matthew 10:16).

Jesus sends us out like sheep among wolves. We may wish Jesus had said, "I'm sending you out like wolves among sheep," but he didn't. We are like sheep among wolves, and we and our children remain vulnerable. Even though Jesus sends us out, he doesn't put a shield around us to protect us from everything evil. We are the wolf bait, not the wolf.

Jesus easily could have said, "Now that you are my followers, separate yourselves from the world." But he didn't. Instead, he said, "I am sending you out . . ." Here's the big idea: *God does not want to take your children out of the world; he wants to take the world out of your children.* God does not want to separate your grown children from the world. Quite the opposite! He wants to send them out into the world to be salt and light. At the same time, he wants them to differ from the world.

All this seems like a pretty tall order! How is it possible? How can a father prepare his children for the world's food chain? We do it by following the advice of Jesus. We do not try to keep our children out of the world, but we do try to keep the world out of them by teaching them some *snake lessons* and some *dove lessons.* With these lessons our children will be able to go *into* the world without becoming *like* the world.

FATHERING THE HEART MEANS TEACHING SNAKE LESSONS

Why do our children need snake lessons? Jesus told his disciples, "Be as shrewd as snakes." Because God will not take our children out of the world, they need to know how to live in the world's system—its food chain—and remain effective for Jesus Christ.

The first lesson our children need to learn is *how to avoid being caught.* Pat and David live in Central Florida, along with ten million snakes! Several times each summer they find snakes in their bushes or grass, even in the suburbs.

Snakes fascinate us. Even though they seem to be everywhere, they wisely avoid natural predators and people. When you do see one, it wants to get away from you just as badly as you want to get away from it. Snakes are very difficult to catch. We have many endangered species of wildlife in Florida, but no snakes among them. They're elusive—they don't get caught!

Cultural predators fill our world, and they are eager to "eat" our children: alcohol, drugs, premarital sex, the pursuit of pleasure, materialism. Our children need to know how to avoid these killers.

Jesus further counsels, "Be on your guard against men" (Matthew 10:17). Worldly predators include more than just sinful activities and ideas; we must also stand guard against people and companies that actively promote an anti-God agenda. These people want to feed on our kids.

We love good rock and roll music. It can stir noble and deep thoughts. It can help us express our innermost feelings. A lot of music, though, is predatory. A VH1 program, for example, showed the one hundred most shocking moments of rock and roll. One infamous clip showed the Red Hot Chili Peppers coming out on stage naked, except for the socks they used to cover their genitalia. And so a legend was born—a legendary band of cultural predators. We shouldn't be shocked. Why should a wolf act like a sheep? We should expect a predator to bite our children if given the chance.

Equip your children with survival training for the food chain. Cultural predators promote a story in competition with the Christian story. Still, we don't suggest that you shield your children from anti-Christian people and ideas. In fact, based on their age and your best discretion, you should expose your children to some of these people and ideas for the purpose of instruction. Watch a movie together and then talk about the values and beliefs presented. Read your children's textbooks and interact with them about the perspective the books champion. Listen to a CD and discuss the lyrics. Help your kids to grow wise about predatory people. If we don't want our kids eaten, we need to help them understand what's really going on. In this way we teach them how to avoid getting caught. We help them to avoid becoming worldly.

FATHERING THE HEART MEANS HELPING YOUR CHILDREN THRIVE IN THE WORLD

Being as shrewd and wise as snakes means more than not getting caught. If it meant no more than that, we could just lock up our children in a monastery. Our kids need to learn a second lesson: *how to survive and thrive in the world.*

Again, Jesus does not want to take our children out of the world. To remain faithful in the world, our kids have to know how to survive and thrive in the world's system—even as they avoid getting caught. Snake lessons also teach our children how to make it in the world.

Think back to the last time you walked through a mall. What word would you use to describe the young people you saw there? Different words and images may come to mind, but one word sums it up for many of these young people: clueless. They are clueless for a reason: No one invests in them and equips them to survive and thrive.

FATHERING THE HEART MEANS IMPARTING A PRACTICAL EDUCATION

What's the best way to help our children get a clue? By giving them a practical education—some snake lessons.

Practical means commonsensical, workable, useful. A practical education moves beyond a theoretical education. What does a practical education look like?

First and foremost, a practical education is biblical. The Bible gives us a lot of wisdom for how to make our way in the world. Scripture commands many things that must be obeyed, prohibits many things that must be avoided, and in between allows many permissible things. But even then, not everything permissible is beneficial.

Men of God compiled the book of Proverbs in ancient times as a manual for parents to give their children a practical education. Proverbs 1:8 declares, for example, "Listen, my son, to your father's instruction ..." The term "my son" appears twenty-three times in Proverbs. (The book mentions sons and not daughters because in that culture only sons received formal instruction in school. But the principles apply to both girls and boys.) Consider a few more examples:

- "My son, if sinners entice you, do not give in to them" (Proverbs 1:10).
- "My son, do not go along with them ..." (Proverbs 1:15).
- "My son, if you accept my words ..., then you will understand the fear of the LORD" (Proverbs 2:1, 5).
- "My son, do not forget my teaching ..." (Proverbs 3:1).
- "My son, do not despise the LORD's discipline ..." (Proverbs 3:11).
- "My son, preserve sound judgment and discernment ..." (Proverbs 3:21).

Proverbs is an impressive manual for instructing children not only in *moral* wisdom but also in the snake lessons of *practical* wisdom. Here are a few examples:

- *Don't talk too much.* "When words are many, sin is not absent, but he who holds his tongue is wise" (Proverbs 10:19).
- *Think before you speak.* "He who guards his lips guards his life, but he who speaks rashly will come to ruin" (Proverbs 13:3).
- *Be careful who you hang out with.* "He who walks with the wise grows wise, but a companion of fools suffers harm" (Proverbs 13:20).
- *Use a gentle word rather than a harsh one.* "A gentle answer turns away wrath, but a harsh word stirs up anger" (Proverbs 15:1).

- *Try to understand others before asking them to understand you.*
  "He who answers before listening—that is his folly and his
  shame" (Proverbs 18:13).
- *Be fair and honest in your work.* "The LORD abhors dishonest
  scales, but accurate weights are his delight" (Proverbs 11:1).
- *Be big enough to "let the little ones go."* "A fool shows his
  annoyance at once, but a prudent man overlooks an insult"
  (Proverbs 12:16).
- *Don't co-sign for someone else's debts.* "He who puts up security
  for another will surely suffer, but whoever refuses to strike
  hands in pledge is safe" (Proverbs 11:15).

May we offer a suggestion to help you father your children's
hearts with a practical education? For the next month, read one
proverb a day to your children and discuss its message. Then give
them an illustration of how it applies—either from your life or a
story you've heard.

FATHERING THE HEART MEANS MENTORING ABOUT WORK, MONEY, AND GETTING ALONG WITH PEOPLE

Snake lessons also apply to the major, everyday issues our children will face. Out of all the areas where we need to mentor children, three stand out: work, money, and getting along with people.

Work is a fulfilling gift from God. Yet, work can also become an
idol. God created us to help shape the culture and contribute to the
world. We need to mentor our children in both the skills and attitudes that will allow them to honor God through their work.

We suggest that, if possible, you take your children to work with
you so they can see what it's like. Develop a system of age-appropriate
chores so your children learn responsibility. Consider taking on a larger
project—adding a room, redoing the floors, rebuilding an engine—
so your children can learn perseverance and determination.

Money is an enabling gift from God. Yet, money also presents a great temptation. It makes promises it cannot keep. Affluence and materialism make a deadly duo, and America is awash in both. We need to teach our children how to use money the way God intended it to be used.

We suggest you teach your children (1) to give 10 percent or more of their allowances to your church and ministries, (2) to save 10 percent of their allowances, (3) to refrain from buying things they don't really need, and (4) to avoid debt. Consider one tip for teaching about debt: Let them borrow money from you for something that will take several weeks to pay back, so they can experience the pain of mortgaging the future for the pleasure of the present.

Getting along with people is a gracious gift from God. Developing a high social intelligence will serve our children throughout life. The better we teach our children how to interact appropriately with others, the greater impact they will have for Christ.

What do we need to teach our children about how to interact with others? We suggest you teach them a few givens: the need to look someone they meet in the eyes; the importance of a firm handshake; the value of smiling often; the benefit of speaking clearly without mumbling. Giving them this confidence in their early years will provide them a valuable head start.

We suggest you teach your kids how to respond to criticism: Listen until the person finishes; let the person know you appreciate hearing a different perspective; and say that you will prayerfully think through what you heard.

We suggest you teach your kids how to receive a compliment, and to enjoy it and say thank you. Teach them how to confront someone gently in love. Teach them how to give constructive criticism while always making it clear they have the person's best interests at heart. Teach them the art of showing appreciation to those who contribute to their lives.

It takes only a few embarrassments or failures to demoralize a child. If we don't properly prepare our children for what they will face, by the time they become teenagers they will begin to shut down and harden their hearts against disappointment and risk.

Conversely, the good news is that it only takes a few successes and encouraging episodes to inspire a child. Teaching our children snake lessons lies at the core of fathering the heart. Snake lessons equip our children to grow wise enough to survive and thrive in the world—without getting caught up in it.

FATHERING THE HEART MEANS TEACHING DOVE LESSONS

As we said earlier, God does not want to take our children out of the world, but he does want to take the world out of our children. And to take the world out of our children we need to teach them some dove lessons.

Dove lessons help our children understand concepts like surrender, submission, not having to have your own way, and not having to win every time. Dove lessons help our children understand that true happiness does not come from getting their own way but from discovering and doing God's will.

At the heart of Jesus' command to be "as innocent as doves" lies the command to consider others more important than yourself. We devote all of chapter 11 ("A Child Who Loves People") to this idea.

If we equipped our children only to be as wise as snakes but missed equipping them to be harmless as doves, our lessons would backfire on us. They may want to become the wolf and not the sheep.

Wisdom without Innocence

Jacob, a junior in high school, knew he had everyone fooled. He kept his grades up, made sure his teachers liked him, and didn't do anything to get on his dad's bad side. The people he worked with at the computer store considered him the greatest. He even went to church with his parents about half the time.

Jacob didn't allow any of them to see the other side of his life. He smoked pot for the first time at a friend's house at age sixteen; now he smoked several times a week. He knew people stupid enough to let pot rule their life, but that wasn't going to happen to him. He stuck to the "rules" he had made, like never smoking at home and never smoking two days in a row. Of course, he broke both of those last night when his parents were gone, but that was just one time. Jacob knew he had a good thing going, and he didn't want to see it all come crashing down.

Jesus tells us, "Be as shrewd as snakes and as innocent as doves." So what does a person look like who is snake-shrewd, but not dove-innocent? He or she is, at best, self-sufficient and, at worst, manipulative and dishonest. Remember Eddie Haskell from *Leave It to Beaver*? That's what he looks like. Our children can learn how to play the game of this world so well that they don't think they need God to succeed. It happens when they grow as shrewd and wise as a snake but not as innocent as a dove.

Innocence without Wisdom

Recently Pat went out to his garage to work. He saw a man and woman drive slowly past, then turn around and come back. The woman got out of the car and said, "Sir, do you know where so-and-so lives?"

"No," Pat said, "I don't think there's anyone on this street by that name."

"We're from Atlanta," the woman replied, "and we are staying at my sister's house. My purse got stolen and the police didn't believe me, and now we need $40 for gas money to get back to Atlanta." By the time she finished, tears were nearly rolling down Pat's face.

"You just wait right here," he told the woman. As he hurried into the house he thought of all the Scriptures he had read and so came back out with $50 inside a copy of *The Man in the Mirror*. By then the woman was sitting in the car with her husband. Pat gave her the book, and she asked, "Have you written other books?"

"As a matter of fact," Pat replied, "I have."

"I think I've got some of your books at home," the woman said. Pat thought, *Oh, bless you, sister!* At about 5:00 P.M. they left.

When Pat got inside he told Patsy what he had done. "You did *what?*" she asked. "They'll be back!"

"Honey," Pat reassured her, "they live in Atlanta, they're down-and-out. Trust me, these are good people—she has some of my books!"

Pat rises early and also tries to go to bed early. At 10:00 P.M. they heard a knock on the door. Patsy turned on the front light, looked through the peephole, then woke Pat to tell him someone was standing at the front door. When Pat peeped through the hole, he saw the woman. Hesitantly he opened the door. She told him their water pump broke just as they pulled onto the interstate highway. Pat, half asleep, didn't follow her story very well. She told him they had used the $50 to get the car fixed and needed $40 more for the gas.

"Wait just a minute," Pat mumbled, shut the door, and got another $40 to give to her. At least he had enough presence of mind to let her know that this was it. "I'm just praying that the Lord will bless us," she said, "and when I get back to Atlanta, I'm going to wire you this money."

When Pat came back inside, Patsy wanted him to explain all the commotion. He described what happened; she just rolled her eyes. The next day Pat realized he probably hadn't acted wisely. He had not applied biblical principles to his decision.

If our children are as innocent as doves but lack wisdom, they will be ineffective and the world will take advantage of them. We need to train our children to remain innocent while still becoming wise.

Dove Lessons for the Tough Times

David served as a student patrol for his elementary school. He was stationed on a sidewalk dangerously close to a narrow street, separated from traffic only by a guardrail. His primary assignment: to make sure the other students stayed on the sidewalk and out of the street.

One afternoon, David set his book bag on one of the posts of the guardrail. About the time his shift ended, a school bully rode his bike down the street. "You need to come over here on the sidewalk," David said, "or I'll have to report you."

The bully stopped his bike, looked David in the eye, and said, "If you report me, I'll beat you up." He kicked David's book bag off the post and rode off down the street. When David got back to school, he reported the student to a teacher.

David rode home, and his mother asked him how school had gone. He told her what had happened and that the bully threatened to beat him up for reporting him. She thought about it for a few moments, then said, "Your older brother, Alan, comes by the end of that road on his bike just before you get out of class. I'll ask him to stop at the end of the road and wait for you to finish your patrol. How does that sound?" It sounded great!

When David reported to his station the next day, he wasn't scared of the bully. Why should he be? He could see Alan waiting for him at the end of the street!

God calls dads to protect their children from bullies, wolves, and predators. When our kids know that we stand "at the end of the street," they will feel the freedom to live as God's sheep. Even more important, when we father the heart and show them that God will work everything out for their good, then they can love God and others with their whole hearts.

Our children can be sheep in a world of wolves only when they have supreme confidence that God will take care of them. And they will trust God more if they see that they can trust us.

God does not want to take your children out of the world, but he does want to take the world out of your children. It takes both wisdom and innocence to love God and others in the world.

THE HEART OF THE MATTER

- Our culture has a food chain, with predators looking to eat our kids.
- How our children fare in the cultural food chain depends on the decisions they make.
- Jesus sends out our children (and us) as vulnerable sheep among the wolves of the world.
- God does not want to take our children out of the world; he wants to take the world out of our children.
- Snake lessons teach our children how to avoid getting caught by the world.
- Snake lessons also teach our children how to thrive in the world.
- Fathering the heart means giving our children a practical education about life.
- We should give our children snake lessons about work, money, and getting along with people.
- Dove lessons "take the world out of our children" by showing them they don't always have to win.
- Wisdom without innocence leads to manipulation and self-sufficiency.
- Innocence without wisdom leads to letting others take advantage of you.
- Children can be sheep in a world of wolves when they know God will take care of them.

TAKE IT TO HEART
QUESTIONS FOR APPLICATION AND DISCUSSION

1. Which way did you grow up: too wise in worldly ways, too naive about the world, or wise enough but still able to maintain your innocence? Has the way you've grown up created problems for you? If so, how?

2. In a sense, our lives are the sum of the decisions we make, some wise and some not. Good decision making provides a major key to your children's success. How can teaching them to be "as wise as snakes and as innocent as doves" help them to make better decisions?

3. What happens if our children end up wise but lose their innocence? Does this seem to be a special risk for your children? If so, what can you do about it?

4. What happens if our children remain innocent but do not become wise? Does this seem a special risk for your children? If so, what can you do about it?

STRAIGHT TO THE HEART
Helping Your Children Discover Their Intelligence

God has designed your children in a special way for a special mission. When you help them find and fulfill their destiny, you will discover one of your great pleasures as a father.

As we have suggested, as a dad you should help your children discover something they do well. One way to father their heart is to help them discover their natural intelligence. Howard Gardner of Harvard University proposed his widely accepted theory of multiple intelligences in his book *Frames of Mind*.[14] Think about your children as you review the eight types of intelligence he identified. Put the initials of each child next to the types of intelligence that apply or may apply to him or her.

____ *Linguistic Intelligence:* Someone with this type of
          intelligence shows unusual sensitivity to the meaning
          and order of words. These folks often become
          language experts, writers, or public speakers.

____ *Logical-Mathematical Intelligence:* This describes an unusual
          ability in math and complex logical systems.
          Someone with this type of intelligence may become a
          computer technologist, engineer, or scientist.

____ *Musical Intelligence:* Someone with this type of intelligence
          has a natural ability to understand and create music.
          Most often they show an interest in being musicians,
          composers, or dancers.

____ *Spatial Intelligence:* This describes the ability to perceive the
          visual world accurately and re-create it or alter it
          mentally or on paper. People with this type of

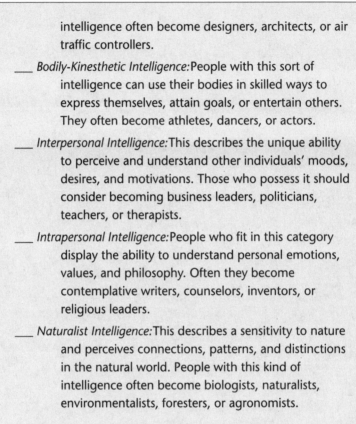

intelligence often become designers, architects, or air traffic controllers.

___ *Bodily-Kinesthetic Intelligence:* People with this sort of intelligence can use their bodies in skilled ways to express themselves, attain goals, or entertain others. They often become athletes, dancers, or actors.

___ *Interpersonal Intelligence:* This describes the unique ability to perceive and understand other individuals' moods, desires, and motivations. Those who possess it should consider becoming business leaders, politicians, teachers, or therapists.

___ *Intrapersonal Intelligence:* People who fit in this category display the ability to understand personal emotions, values, and philosophy. Often they become contemplative writers, counselors, inventors, or religious leaders.

___ *Naturalist Intelligence:* This describes a sensitivity to nature and perceives connections, patterns, and distinctions in the natural world. People with this kind of intelligence often become biologists, naturalists, environmentalists, foresters, or agronomists.

Exploring and developing your children's natural intelligence will help empower them to fulfill God's calling on their lives.

Look over the list. Are you allowing your children to get involved in activities that will expand and make use of their particular kind of intelligence? For each of your children, try to think of one activity you can help them pursue that seems appropriate for each of the intelligence types you suspect that God has given them.

CHAPTER 7

Helping Children
Get Their Story Straight

David attended a liberal arts university with a Christian heritage. By the 1980s, when David attended college, the school had professors who represented the gamut of religious and philosophical thought, with evangelical Christianity definitely in the minority.

Unfortunately, many parents have sent their children to this "Christian" school unprepared to face the philosophical and religious challenges it presented. One of the most painful experiences of David's life was watching freshmen who seemed to love Christ become juniors who wanted nothing to do with God.

FATHERING THE HEART REQUIRES
KNOWING WHAT STORIES ARE OUT THERE

Author Neil Postman says, "Human beings need stories to give meaning to the facts of their existence."[15] We need meaningful "stories" to make sense of our world. A story is a set of fundamental ideas or beliefs that provides a filter through which we can sift the bits and pieces of our lives. Some call this story a worldview, a system, or a metanarrative.

All stories believed by rational people claim to explain human suffering and human happiness. If a story did not have some degree of plausibility and believability, nobody would listen to it. Nobody gives their life to a story or a system they don't think works. And yet many adults wake up one day in their thirties, forties, fifties, or sixties, and realize they have been giving their lives to a system that offers no possibility of making them happy.

What stories dominate our culture today? What competes with the Christian story for the allegiance of our children? Pat outlined the following stories in his book for high school boys, *The Young Man in the Mirror*, which he adapted from Postman and Mardi Keyes.[16]

The Story of the American Dream

Remember when your third grade teacher told you that someone in the class might grow up to be president one day? That's the American Dream. If you believe it, you can achieve it. There is nothing you can't do with enough hard work. If you want to be happy, just get a good education, a well-paying job, a nice house, and you will have a good life. This is the dominant story of the baby boomer generation. Many children still latch on to this story today. A teacher in a suburban high school recently said, "One of my biggest challenges is, what can I do to help students who have been drilled by their parents that they can do whatever they want—even though they obviously lack aptitude?"

The Story of Human Progress

The idea of human progress dominated the twentieth century. It says that man is basically good and we can solve all the problems of the world if we just try harder and all work together. After two world wars, Hitler, Stalin, Vietnam, and genocide on every continent, the story of the perfectibility of man no longer seems a serious position. Still, the idea of human goodness exerts a powerful pull on society, especially in government and education. Musicians who invite your children to concerts for world hunger, AIDS, and farm relief often also champion this message.

The Story of Technological Paradise

Americans love technology. We constantly look for the next gadget to make our lives easier. Many people live with the hope that machines will ultimately solve the problems that humans couldn't solve, like world hunger or world peace. Today a whole generation really thinks that we're going to come up with a high-tech paradise. Our children can be lured into thinking that technology will do for them what only Christ can do.

The Story of Postmodernism

We live in what many call a postmodern world—a world of no absolute truths. Many intellectuals have built a philosophy around the meaninglessness and futility of life. They see no inherent meaning to life, only the meaning that we bring to it through our own efforts. This philosophy, called nihilism, has made its way into popular culture through music and movies. Nihilism has become the dominant story on many college campuses today. Because everything is futile, it only makes sense to get as much as you can.

Pat's daughter interned for a campus ministry for two years at a public university. She befriended a girl who had grown up in the home of a devout Christian mother and a violent father. Her parents divorced at a young age. This young woman attended the campus ministry meeting every week for two years, as well as participating in a small group Bible study with Pat's daughter. One day she said (Pat realizes that this may sound offensive, but this is what she said), "Jen, I believe in God, but I think he sucks."

This illustrates the essence of the story of futility that many children are learning. Dads truly need to understand this story, because if you don't explain and debunk it while your kids are still living at home, they will get completely rattled in college.

The Story of Science

On one hand, the story of science tells us everything that exists is essentially a cosmic accident, the result of evolution and chance. On the other hand, science offers "meaning" and "hope" by providing answers that explain how the universe works. It tries to explain everything by natural cause and effect, so it has no place for supernatural intervention and, therefore, no God. Of course, this doesn't offer much explanation for things like love and suffering—so, in the end, this story feels emotionally unsatisfying to most people.

Your sons and daughters will hear that they evolved from ape-like creatures and that everything is chance. As fathers, we have an opportunity to show our children a much, much bigger reason for our existence.

The Story of Spiritualism and New Age

As a reaction to the inability of science to meet our deepest needs, a new spirituality developed in the West. With an emphasis on angels, spirit guides, communicating with the dead, and Eastern mysticism, this could be called "the anti-science."

This story asks us to go beyond what science or reason tells us. We are summoned to enter the world of the spirit, where what we believe helps determine what is real. Men and women get in touch with their own "spirituality" in order to discover how to become authentic persons. Many scholars foresee an increase in spiritual things in the decades ahead—but not necessarily distinctly Christian.

Fathers can protect their children's hearts by explaining and discussing all religions, then showing their children the superiority of the Christian story. (Pat's book *Coming Back to God* explains the superiority of Christianity.[17])

The Story of Consumerism

Many of us are intimately familiar with this "yuppie" tale. Consumerism is the economic theory that an increasingly greater consumption of goods is beneficial. Our American economy runs on this philosophy. If the Gross Domestic Product increases from one year to the next, everyone feels happy and assumes we are better off. If production decreases or stagnates, it spells trouble.

But, of course, if we produce more goods and services, then someone has to consume them. So we are encouraged—no, inspired!—to believe that having increasingly more things will bring us increasing happiness. We want to acquire enough stuff to make us secure and comfortable and to avoid suffering. This story of consumerism and materialism strongly tempts our children. As dads, we have a golden opportunity to father our children's hearts not to find their satisfaction in "things."

All of these stories appeal to the mind of a child because each attempts to give a reasonable explanation for the world we see. But, even more important, they appeal to our children's hearts by offering a sense of meaning, purpose, fun, adventure, or worth. Everyone ends up giving his or her heart to some story. As fathers we must help our children choose a story worth living for.

FATHERING THE HEART MEANS PROTECTING FROM THE WRONG STORY

One day as Pat rode around in his car he noticed a slight odor. A few days went by, and it seemed that each day the odor increased. Pretty soon it began to drive him crazy. Another few days went by, and it started to smell like a dead animal.

While Pat doesn't consider himself a very mechanical person, he started looking around the car and thought maybe the problem came from the trunk. He looked there but couldn't find anything. Then he thought perhaps something crawled up in the engine and died, so he looked all around the engine but still couldn't find it.

Finally, after two weeks the smell was really horrible. Pat decided he had to take his car apart, piece by piece. After twenty minutes of looking around the interior of the car for the tenth time, Pat leaned over in the back seat and noticed little pouches on the backs of the front seat. He looked in the pouch directly behind the driver's seat and found a plastic sandwich bag with a half-eaten, green sandwich his son had left behind several weeks earlier.

It took another month to get rid of the beastly smell.

A lot of the stories we adopt to explain our lives resemble that sandwich. The story looks good in the beginning and may even work for a while (twenty years or more), but eventually it begins to rot. Not only do these false stories fail us in this life, but, more important, they fail us in the life to come. To father the hearts of our children means to protect them from the wrong stories.

FATHERING THE HEART MEANS UNDERSTANDING WHY STORIES ATTRACT FOLLOWERS

Why did such stories gain such great popularity in our culture? Each one offers three attractive features.

1. Plausibility

As one of Pat's professors said, "It takes a lot of truth to float an error." If these stories contained no truth, only completely irrational people would believe them. So these stories will offer some ring of truth to your children, as perhaps they have to you. All stories that make it in our popular culture have some degree of plausibility.

2. Promise

All of these stories implicitly or explicitly promise an explanation for human suffering and offer to provide the happiness that seems to elude everyone else. Even stories based in meaninglessness and despair promise to explain reality. They promise something to satisfy the longings of the heart.

3. Prophets

All of these stories boast impressive spokesmen and "evangelists" who articulate the tenets of the story. They also have "priests" who administer the sacraments, if you will, of the story. They have people who deeply believe it and so go out to sell the story to others, and they all have disciples and followers who want others to join them.

So our children get introduced to one of these stories—usually by an adult they admire and trust. In the beginning, the story looks and sounds really good. Their friends go down the same path, famous people tout these ideas, and their teachers try to convince them what is true. As they consider a story, they seem to find answers there to questions they have been asking, perhaps even unconsciously.

FATHERING THE HEART MEANS HELPING CHILDREN UNDERSTAND HOW STORIES DECEIVE

Many of the followers of these stories seem to be finding success. So our children look at them and experience what the psalmist writes about: "My feet were slipping, and I was almost gone. For I envied the proud, when I saw them prosper despite their wickedness" (Psalm 73:2–3 NLT). Many people who follow the world's stories appear to be doing well on the outside. Psalm 73 continues:

> They seem to live such a painless life;
> > their bodies are so healthy and strong.
> They aren't troubled like other people
> > or plagued with problems like everyone else.
> They wear pride like a jeweled necklace,
> > and their clothing is woven of cruelty.
> These fat cats have everything
> > their hearts could ever wish for!
> They scoff and speak only evil;
> > in their pride they seek to crush others.
> They boast against the very heavens,
> > and their words strut throughout the earth.
> And so the people are dismayed and confused,
> > drinking in all their words.
> "Does God realize what is going on?" they ask.
> > "Is the Most High even aware of what is happening?"
>
> Psalm 73:4–11 NLT

When Clark graduated from college, he went to work selling large-ticket copy machines. The sales manager dazzled Clark with his new BMW, gold watch, expensive restaurants, great clothes, and beautiful home. It seemed a dream—the American Dream—and Clark got hooked. He told his wife, "This is the answer! This is how we can have a happy life and avoid the money problems so many of our friends have." Of course, Clark couldn't see the huge monthly payments needed to keep it all afloat and the constant bickering with his sales manager and with his wife over money. Clark didn't see this because he hadn't had a father who helped him get his story straight.

We need to start early with our kids. Like most children, David's kids saw commercials on TV enticing them to ask for the latest toys and games. When they asked for one of the toys, he engaged them in a conversation about the message behind the commercial:

"Why do you want the Astro-Blaster 9200X?"

"Because it's cool and it obliterates stuff with a big, huge bang."

"Were the children happy or sad in the commercial when they were playing with the toy?"

"They were happy."

"Is this commercial trying to make you think you need an Astro-Blaster to be happy?"

"Yes."

"Do you think you can still be happy even if you never get an Astro-Blaster?"

"Yes."

"I'm glad you want an Astro-Blaster, and Mommy and Daddy will think about that. It looks like it could be a lot of fun. But we also want you to remember that the toys we have are not what make us happy. God makes us happy when we love him and love other people."

This may seem idealized (though something like it really did happen!), but we need to help our children think clearly about the overwhelming tide of information forced on them by our culture. We must help them interpret movies, their academics, their athletic goals, the books they read, the magazines they read, and the expectations of their peers. We need to help them get their story straight.

FATHERING THE HEART MEANS ANSWERING OUR CHILDREN'S QUESTIONS

Children have a knack for asking profound questions. "Dad, where do babies come from?" "Daddy, how come Grandpa had to die?" "Dad, I tried to be honest, yet I was the one the teacher sent to the principal's office. Why would God let that happen?" "Dad, if I share my toys with Sally just so that I can have treasures in heaven, is that being selfish?"

Even though children have a way of asking these questions at awkward moments, their questions present us with some of our best "teaching moments" to father the hearts of our children.

Underneath these questions often lie deeper questions about life, death, happiness, meaning, purpose, and significance. Our children may never put many of these questions into words—they probably couldn't find the right words even if they wanted to. But this doesn't make them any less real. It may mean they represent something even more important.

We all have times when something bothers us, but we can't quite put our finger on the problem. The questions our children ask point to these deeper, heart questions that every person asks: "Why am I here?" "Is there a God?" "Is he good?" "Does he care about me?" "Can I make my life count?" C. S. Lewis said in *Mere Christianity*, "If I find in myself a desire which no experience in this world can satisfy, the most probable explanation is that I was made for another world."[18]

FATHERING THE HEART MEANS EQUIPPING WITH A STORY THAT IS PLAUSIBLE AND TRUE

Our children need a story that is not only plausible but true. And our children need a story that is not only true but plausible.

At a wedding a few years ago Pat ran into an old friend. They had known each other for a very long time. Pat considers him one of the finest men he has ever known. The man has squeaky-clean morals and incredible integrity. He looks good, has a lot of money, and even married into a family with a lot of money. He's basically a poster child for human progress and the American Dream.

He and Pat had a delightful conversation. Pat said to him, "You know, I've always admired you very much, and I just wish our paths would have crossed more over the years. I would love to have spent more time together."

"You know," the man said, "I feel the same way."

After a few more minutes, Pat brought the conversation to an end and started to move away. But the way the man looked at Pat— you could just see the loneliness in his eyes. He stopped Pat and said, "Do you think we could get together and have lunch sometime?" This man had found worldly success but hadn't had a father who helped him get his story straight.

The problem is that all stories except Christianity come to nothing. They may be plausible, but they are not true. So in the end people give their lives to a "story" that lets them down. It can't keep its promises.

It's not enough for a story to be plausible; it also has to be true. Christianity has an incredible advantage over all other stories because it is true. Sadly, many young people today do not see Christianity even as a serious option. They simply can't bring themselves to believe Christianity is true because they can't believe it's plausible. So they're dropping out. Dallas Seminary professor Howard Hendricks says that four out of five children will drop out of church by the time they become seniors in high school. Why? For one thing, they are not receiving enough evidence from their parents and peers to see that Christianity is a viable option for life.

FATHERING THE HEART MEANS GETTING OUR OWN STORY STRAIGHT

So what can a father do? First, we have to get our own story straight. A lot of us have been giving the best years of our lives to a story that isn't true, and now we are passing this story along to our children. Our children will inherit the story that we live out, just as the Bible says in Deuteronomy 6. They will soak in the story that we communicate as they sit at home, as they walk along the road, as they lie down, and as they get up. Our children will adopt the story that we live out every day.

Equip yourself to interpret the stories of our culture and evaluate them biblically. Why not reread and study the stories we mentioned above, with your own story in mind? Read your Bible regularly to counter the lies of this world. Get into relationships with other men where you can be discipled and encouraged to grow. Commit yourself to a church where you can have a significant impact for the kingdom of God. All of these things will help you get your story straight so that you can father the hearts of your children.

As fathers we need to passionately commit our hearts to Christ alone. We must come to the cross of Jesus Christ and negotiate a full and complete surrender to him. We have to ruthlessly and continuously abandon any other "gods" that we imagine can satisfy our souls. This is repentance, and this is what it means to get our story straight.

If you don't get your own story straight, how will you give your children something you don't have? Too many of us have one story on Sunday, one story on Monday morning, and then a different story at the dinner table. Let's have one story, let's get it straight, and let's show that story to our kids. In the end they will see the story of Christianity as not only plausible but true.[19] We cannot overstate the crucial importance of getting our story right. The eternal destiny and temporal peace of our children depend on it.

THE HEART OF THE MATTER

- A "story" is a worldview or system that explains the world.
- Some dominant stories in our culture include the American Dream, human progress, technological paradise, postmodernism, science, spiritualism and New Age, and consumerism.
- Fathering the heart means helping our children reject the wrong stories.
- All stories that make it in the cultural food chain have plausibility, promise, and prophets.
- Our children need a story that is both plausible and true.
- Our children will inherit the story we live out.
- It takes effort to fully understand the Christian story and pass it on to our children.

TAKE IT TO HEART
QUESTIONS FOR APPLICATION AND DISCUSSION

1. What story did you grow up believing? (Look back through the chapter section headings.) If not the Christian story, when and how did you realize your story wouldn't work?

2. Identify the story of the man described in Psalm 73:1–9. When it seems as though his story is working, what does that do to us, according to verses 10–16, 21? But how does the story end, according to verses 17–20?

3. What story have you been most tempted to believe as an adult, and why? How has this affected the choices you have

made in your life? What steps do you need to take to get your *own* story straight?

4. Which story do you think particularly tempts your children? Why do you think it appeals to his or her heart? What specific steps can you take to engage your child about the shortcomings of this story?

5. What have you told your children about the Christian story? What other stories have you mentioned to them? How have you explained the differences between these stories and shown them the superiority of Christianity? What else do you need to do? What's your next step?

STRAIGHT TO THE HEART
Foundational Truths Every Child Should Understand

God calls every father to become a spiritual leader for his children. One of the most effective ways to father your children's hearts is to disciple them to understand who God really is.

Too many adults have a relationship with God but know almost nothing about him. Since they don't know what they believe, they are "blown here and there by every wind of teaching and by the cunning and craftiness of men in their deceitful scheming" (Ephesians 4:14). What happens after a few years of this? As adults, a lot of them ask themselves, "Why did I ever believe this in the first place?" and end up chucking it all.

As a father, what can you do to help prevent this? You can lay a foundation to demonstrate that Christianity answers the deepest questions of life. Consider a few basic truths about God and his Word that can serve as a starting point for your children.[20]

The Trinity. Since the formulation of the Nicene Creed in A.D. 325, the church has spoken of God as "three persons in one essence." This means that, though we believe in only one God, he exists in three persons, all of whom equally share the essence of God. The Father is God, Jesus is God, and the Holy Spirit is God. They work together as a team in creation and redemption. But while the doctrine of the Trinity safeguards the truth, it does not fully explain it.

The doctrine of the Trinity helps our children answer questions like, "What is God really like?" "Why am I so desperate for relationships?" and "How did the world begin?"

God the Son. Jesus is God, just like the Father and the Holy Spirit. He has existed from eternity but became a man two thousand years ago to redeem his people from their sins. His perfect life fulfilled the demands of the law for people who could never do it on their own. His death paid the penalty for the sins of all those who place their faith and trust in him.

The truth about Jesus helps our children answer questions like, "I know I am guilty before God, but what can I do?" "How can I ever be good enough for God to love me?" and "Is there anyone who will ever love me just for me?"

God the Holy Spirit. The Holy Spirit is God. That makes him a person, not an it. He lives in every person who has trusted Christ by faith. He encourages, comforts, convicts, heals, guides, and intercedes for us. God gave him to us as a down payment of what it will be like one day to live in the presence of God forever.

The doctrine of the Holy Spirit helps our children answer questions like, "Will God take care of me?" "How can I know God's will?" and "Will God always be with me?"

The Bible. Godly men wrote the Bible under the inspiration of the Holy Spirit. Through the Bible God reveals himself to mankind. In the Bible, God tells us everything we need to know to have a fulfilling relationship with him. It does not answer all our questions, nor does it seem equally clear on every point. Still, as the Word of God, it has proven to be a reliable guide to faith and life.

The doctrine of Scripture helps our children answer questions like, "Is there really any absolute truth?" "How can we know anything about God anyway?" and "How can I know what God wants me to do?"

Prayer. God created us for a relationship with him. Prayer serves as the currency of our relationship with God, and we should spend it liberally. Even though God rules sovereignly over all creation, prayer really does change things. Prayer unleashes spiritual power into the physical world.

The doctrine of prayer helps our children answer questions like, "How do I talk to God?" and "Will God listen to me?"

The Church. The church is the family and flock of God. It is the new community and represents a taste of the kingdom of heaven. We should invest ourselves in a local church and use our gifts to impact others for Christ. Every person needs to actively grow and serve in a local church.

The doctrine of the church helps our children answer questions like, "Where is God at work in the world?" "Where can I use the gifts and talents God has given me?" and "How should I handle the money and resources I've received from God?"

Baptism. Denominations differ on their interpretation of baptism, but all agree on its importance. Given as a sign and seal of the new covenant, baptism represents an important step in following Jesus. Some churches baptize infants by sprinkling, others baptize only believers by immersion. Make it a point to find out what your church believes about baptism and why.

The doctrine of baptism helps our children answer questions like, "What does it mean to follow Jesus?" and "What is the significance of Jesus' life and death for me?"

Communion. Jesus himself instituted the Lord's Supper on the night before his crucifixion. Based largely on the Old Testament Passover, this meal allows us to remember what Jesus has done and enables us to look forward to the day we will eat with him in heaven. The bread signifies his body given for us on the cross; the wine signifies his blood shed for us. Communion allows us to spiritually feast on and with Jesus by faith.

The doctrine of the Lord's Supper helps our children answer questions like, "Why did Jesus die?" "What did his death do for me?" and "What is the hope that I have in heaven?"

These key doctrines can help form a solid foundation for a life of faith. Why not make it a point to interact with your children about these ideas over the next few weeks—perhaps take one per week on a set day? Helping them know why they believe what they believe forms a key component of fathering your children's hearts.

CHAPTER 8

Growing a Heart of Faith in Your Child

Pat sat down one day and intentionally asked, "What is the single most important thing I can do for my children?" It only took him a few minutes to fill a page of notes about what might give his kids the greatest likelihood of happiness, success, meaning, and purpose in life.

As he scanned his long list, something didn't seem right. Finally he crumpled it up and threw it away. "The single most important thing I can do for my children," he concluded, "is to help them develop a heart for God."

When we talk about discipling the hearts of our children to love God, we are not talking merely about our children becoming Christians but about seeing them come to enjoy Jesus and have a passion to glorify him. We can do nothing better for our children than to help them realize their only hope for authentic meaning lies in the gospel of Jesus Christ.

FATHERING THE HEART MEANS DISCIPLING A HEART FOR GOD

We already have said that too often we dads focus on the *behavior* we hope to see in our children. We want them to get a good education, find a good job, be respectful and polite, have good relationships with their friends, and so on. But what does the Bible say about these things? It says these things flow out of a heart of faith.

Acts 13:22 describes a better hope for our children: "[God] testified concerning [David]: 'I have found David son of Jesse a man after my own heart; he will do everything I want him to do.'" The Lord called David a man after God's own heart—not a perfect man, but a man willing to do whatever God called him to do.

What a wonderful tribute for God to give *your* children! Any Christian father would love to have children willing to do whatever God wants them to do. But this will happen only if our children develop a heart of love for God.

FATHERING THE HEART MEANS MAKING THE MAIN THING THE MAIN THING

"Will my children stay true to the Christian faith?" A survey of Christian parents named that question as their number one concern. Yet we have seen that only 60 percent of those who grow up in evangelical churches remain there as adults.[21]

What an incredible disparity! The most important concern of Christian fathers is the very thing that's not happening. What kind of investment can we make now to help our children develop a heart for God that will last a lifetime?

Fathers have no magic formulas to turn out godly kids. At the same time, children reared in a family where the gospel of grace is loved and lived out will, in the vast majority of cases, come to love God for themselves. We can't make our children love God, but we can put them in the way of falling more in love with Jesus. We can create an environment where they see the benefits of loving Jesus.

How can you make "a heart for God" appealing to your kids? Consider three practical things you can do as a father, and then we'll look at three practical things you can help your children do.

FATHERING THE HEART MEANS PRAYING DAILY FOR YOUR CHILDREN

The first and most practical thing you can do is pray. Don't think, *I guess the only thing I can do is pray,* but, *the best thing I can do is pray.*

Derrick seemed like a pretty normal kid. Sure, he rebelled in high school and did a few dumb things, but no more than most other kids. After high school, though, Derrick faltered. He made no plans. He meandered like a river without banks. He spilled out in every direction. With too much time on his hands, Derrick started hanging with a group of guys who lived on the edge. Derrick started doing drugs and got arrested.

When his father, Jeff, received that late-night call from the police, it didn't take him completely by surprise. He had felt helpless as he watched his son sink. Whenever Jeff pictured his son, he saw a cute little eight-year-old who followed him around like a puppy. Now his son had passed his twentieth birthday, and Jeff had watched each of his hopes and dreams for his boy go up in smoke. *Where did I go wrong?* he wondered. No pain compares to child pain.

Jeff and his wife wept themselves into exhaustion that night. Then they prayed. They enlisted an army of friends and acquaintances to pray too. Jeff never gave up hope that through prayer, Christ would prevail in his son's life. Several turbulent years followed, but eventually Derrick surrendered his life to Christ and today is slowly making progress.

We pray you will never have to endure "child pain" as deeply as Jeff. But if you do, through prayer God will make a way where there just doesn't seem to be a way. And even if our children don't fall into all-out rebellion, all of us will face challenges too big to handle without God's help. So we encourage you to make prayer for your children a regular habit.

Think about this: You and your wife probably are the only two people in the world willing to regularly pray for your children. You should pray, because your children never move beyond God's reach. Prayer is hard work—but it is the only work that brings the power of the kingdom of God into our human actions.

Pat has previously published the list he has used to pray for his own children.[22] In case you've never seen it, here it is again. He asks the Lord . . .

- that there will never be a time they don't walk with the Lord
- for a saving faith (thanksgiving if they already are Christians)
- for a growing faith
- for an independent faith (as they grow up)
- for persevering faith
- that they will be strong and healthy in mind, body, and spirit
- for a sense of destiny (purpose)
- for a desire for integrity
- for a call to excellence
- that they might understand their spiritual gifts
- that they might understand the ministry God has for them
- for godly values and beliefs—a Christian worldview
- that they might tithe 10 percent and save 10 percent of all earnings
- that they might set and work toward realistic goals as revealed by the Lord
- that I will set aside times to spend with them
- that they might acquire wisdom
- for protection from drugs, alcohol, tobacco, premarital sex, violence, rape, and AIDS
- for the mate God has for them (alive somewhere, needing prayer)
- that they might do daily devotions
- for forgiveness and to be filled with the Holy Spirit
- any personal requests or matters in discussion with their mother
- that they might glorify the Lord in everything

FATHERING THE HEART MEANS TEACHING YOUR CHILDREN THE CHRISTIAN STORY

We need to instruct our children into a Christian worldview, or "story." This relates to the idea of the previous chapter—*getting our story straight*. How exactly would you do that? You might summarize the Christian story for your kids by tutoring them around five key concepts: God, Creation, the Fall, Redemption, and the New Creation. These five ideas will go a long way toward explaining what your children will experience in their lives.

God. Start with the story about God. In order for children to make sense of the little bits and pieces of their lives, they need to understand who God is. Jesus is God, the foundation for everything that exists. His holiness sets the standard for moral purity. His power underlies all the forces of nature. His self-existence provides the ground for the existence of the universe. We find ultimate meaning only in relationship to Jesus. Teach your children to appreciate the greatness of God and to desire a relationship with Jesus.

Creation. God made the world from nothing, and he made it perfect. When God had finished creating the world, it suffered from no sin or sorrow or sickness or death. Understanding this will encourage our children to appreciate the goodness and greatness of God.

The Fall. The saddest part of the story—but the part that most helps us understand why things went so haywire—is the Fall. Into God's perfect world, sin and evil entered through Adam and Eve's sin. So now we live in a broken world, a world shattered by futility. Our children need to grasp that ultimately the world will always disappoint them and let them down. This isn't the way God meant things to be, but sin has fouled up everything. This will encourage our children to put their hope and trust in Jesus. Pascal has called the Fall an offense to human reason, but once accepted, he observed, it makes perfect sense of the human condition.[23]

Redemption. If the world as we see it were the end of the story, what a depressing ending it would be. But a glorious thing happened two thousand years ago when God entered this evil world as an innocent child, lived a perfect life, gained victory over sin, and died as a sacrifice for the sins of all those who put their faith and trust in him. Jesus guarantees salvation to all who will turn to him in faith and repentance. Our children need to be encouraged to trust in Jesus for the redemption he offers.

New Creation. The best stories always have a great ending, and the Christian story is no exception. Yes, our children must live in a world riddled with the effects of the Fall. Yet this world also has what Francis Schaeffer called "leftover beauty." So into our lives comes a mixture of blessing and curse. We taste the goodness of God and have the Holy Spirit with us, but we also suffer for our own sins and the sins of others. We eagerly await the day of our final "adoption as sons" (Romans 8:23). Teaching this to our children will encourage them to persevere and to believe that they will prevail.

These few truths will help your child interpret nearly everything that happens to them in life. How important is this? The psalmist wrote this:

> O my people, hear my teaching;
>> listen to the words of my mouth.
> I will open my mouth in parables,
>> I will utter hidden things, things from of old—
> what we have heard and known,
>> what our fathers have told us.
> We will not hide them from their children;
>> we will tell the next generation
> the praiseworthy deeds of the LORD,
>> his power, and the wonders he has done.
> He decreed statutes for Jacob
>> and established the law in Israel,
> which he commanded our forefathers
>> to teach their children,
> so the next generation would know them,
>> even the children yet to be born,

and they in turn would tell their children.
Then they would put their trust in God
and would not forget his deeds
but would keep his commands.
They would not be like their forefathers—
a stubborn and rebellious generation,
whose hearts were not loyal to God,
whose spirits were not faithful to him.

Psalm 78:1–8

God always intended that fathers pass on the knowledge of God to the next generation. Many otherwise wonderful fathers really miss the boat at this point. Pat's dad was one of them.

Like many fathers, Pat's dad delegated the spiritual instruction of his children to others. Pat's parents took him and his three brothers to church, but they didn't explain how Christianity connected to real life. By the time Pat started high school in the early 1960s, his family had stopped attending church altogether. Pat had great parents overall, but their spiritual lapse amounted to a huge mistake. Their decision threw his entire family into a long, downward spiral from which the family barely recovered. All four boys lost their spiritual bearings.

Without instruction about God, Pat and his brothers had no purpose, no sense of identity. So they floundered: Pat for six years; Robert for twenty years until his death in 1983; Pete until 1994; and Bill will have to speak for himself, but Pat thinks he is searching. The simple act of not going to church pulled the plug on what could have been a great family heritage. Instead, they wound up with a lot of shattered lives.

By contrast, David's father modeled faith in Christ and instructed his children in the Christian faith. Church was always a priority, and David saw his father teach classes and serve in leadership roles. His dad encouraged David and his brothers to get involved in youth activities and mission trips. His parents told others about Christ and demonstrated Christ's love in tangible ways. David's father and mother sacrificed to give generously for church building programs and missionary work. In short, David's dad and mom let their faith influence every area of their lives.

Today David and his two brothers all have remained active in their local churches and other ministries. Each of them has served in leadership roles and had a hand in influencing others to follow Christ. And all three are praying and working to pass on the faith to the next generation.

How striking to compare our two stories side by side! Both of us had great dads, moral dads, hardworking dads, and Christian dads. The difference? David's dad discipled him to love God and others from the heart. It still mystifies Pat why his parents would pull the plug on church. It made his search for God so much longer and so much more painful than it needed to be.

FATHERING THE HEART MEANS MODELING YOUR LOVE FOR CHRIST

Andrew Carnegie once said, "As I grow older, I pay less attention to what men say. I just watch what they do." That's what children often do too. They may not pay attention to what we say, but they see everything we do. Our children watch us! And that's why you have to model your Christian faith before your children. Children learn more from what they see than from what they hear. As Edgar Guest once said, "I'd rather see a sermon than to hear one any day."

Because of this, we believe that every dad should have two goals:

- a one-to-one correlation between his public and private life
- the humility to admit his failures

One reason why four out of five kids drop out of church is that they see a disconnect in their father's faith. Their dads don't model humility and moment-by-moment dependence on God's grace. Ask yourself, "Do my children see me making decisions based on the principles of God's Word? Do they see me sacrificing short-term pleasure for the long-term blessing of serving Christ? Do they hear my prayers as I ask God to be glorified in my life?"

David's nine-year-old daughter recently had a tough time, whining off and on for several hours. Finally David had had enough. Out of frustration, he listened to her but intentionally put a look of mock concern on his face.

She was crushed. She felt belittled and humiliated and immediately ran to her room in tears. David knew exactly what to do—at least in part because he was working on this book. After a few minutes, he went to his daughter's room and confessed his sin to her. He told her that he had acted in a mean and wrong way and that he had asked God to change his heart. She forgave him and learned something from his vulnerability.

Every dad will hurt his children—it takes a man to admit it.

Pray for your kids, instruct them about God and Christ, and then model for them what you would like them to become. Perhaps you've heard it said, "We teach what we believe, but we reproduce what we are."

Now let's turn from what you can do as a dad to what your children can do for themselves.

FATHERING THE HEART MEANS HAVING YOUR CHILDREN JOIN YOU IN CHURCH

Whatever you do, get your kids to church. Force them if you must. Sound too strong? Please hear out our reasoning. You may chafe on this point, perhaps because of your own experience. You may have been forced to go to church as a child, or perhaps you have suffered a negative experience trying to force your own kids to go to church.

But what if we asked you, "Do you think you should force your children to go to school even if they don't want to go to school?" Of course you would say, "Yes."

What if we said, "What if they don't like school and the only reason they learn is because we force them to go?" What would you say? You would probably think we had lost our marbles.

"Who cares if they don't like it! They need it!" That's what you would say, right? So we have to ask: Is church any less important than school?

Pat often wonders what would have become of his family had his parents kept everyone in church. He'll never know. He knows only that soon after dropping out, his family began to implode.

It takes time to become a mature disciple of Jesus Christ—a long time. Usually it happens only when we get involved in relationships with others who are on the same journey. Where does that happen? In church. Church is the most dependable place where your children will develop Christian friends, learn about God and what he has done, get exposed to meaningful youth activities, and hear the gospel of Jesus Christ. If they're not in church, who will reinforce what you teach them? If you do not require your children to attend church, you put them at great risk.

How can you require them to be in church? Simply make the consequences of not being in church unacceptable. What do they want to do so badly that losing the privilege would cause them to make sure they attended church?

Pat once had a conflict with his daughter over her curfew. She wanted to stay out later on Saturday nights. Finally, Pat and Patsy thought she was old enough to stay out later so they adjusted the curfew a bit. Sure enough, the next morning she couldn't get up in time for her youth activities at church.

As you can imagine, this started an escalating conflict. Pat and Patsy told her she couldn't go out the next Saturday night because she missed church. Immediately, the conversation turned to Pat and his actions. "You're not letting me grow up. I've got to learn to make my own decisions."

So instead of making it their choice, Pat and Patsy said, "Okay, we'll make this into a simple rule. You can go out on Saturday nights and keep the new curfew, but you have to be up for church on Sunday morning. If you miss a Sunday, then the following Saturday night you can't go out. Does that sound fair to you?" She agreed that it did.

You can probably guess how many times she slept in on Sunday morning. Once. After she owned the responsibility for the consequences—and felt the pain!—it never happened again.

How long should you force your children to go to church? We recommend you do so as long as they remain under your direct authority as a father.

FATHERING THE HEART MEANS IMPRESSING THE IMPORTANCE OF MISSIONS AND SERVICE

Most young people in our culture have little opportunity to feel the weight of poverty, oppression, and despair. You can help your children develop a heart for God by encouraging their involvement in missions and service.

Pat's son, John, went on a mission trip to Mexico to help build a church. Before he left he purchased a pair of leather work gloves. Working side by side with several Mexican laborers, he developed a love for the Mexican people and an appreciation for their faith in the midst of poverty. He couldn't believe how little they had to work with! When he left, he gave his leather gloves to a man with whom he had bonded. You would have thought John had given the man a thousand dollars!

What happens when your children see people of great faith living in difficult circumstances? It encourages them to put their own hope in God. Helping a person in need gives them a greater sense of God's purpose.

Your children can get involved in a mercy ministry through your church. Join them if possible. Go to the homeless shelter and serve food, work on a house with Habitat for Humanity, do yard work for a widow in the congregation—there are lots of relatively easy ways to help your children think about something bigger than themselves.

Many local churches offer short-term missions opportunities for middle and high school students. National organizations also sponsor trips. Whether it's a visit to an impoverished area of the United States or a trip to a foreign country, a mission trip will help expand the vision of your children.

Of course, you don't always have to "go." Pat's family often invited visiting missionaries and Christian speakers to stay with them or have dinner with them. Their children caught a much bigger vision for the world because of those times.

FATHERING THE HEART MEANS ENCOURAGING YOUR CHILDREN TO SPEND TIME WITH GOD

A regular time of devotions helps your children develop a heart for God. We suggest that you do this as a family and also help your kids have their own private devotions.

Pat's family, for example, did a fifteen-minute family Bible study and prayer time three or four days a week in the morning before school. Pat would try to come up with an interesting question or a quote to hook his children, read a Bible verse, give them a principle, tell an illustration or a story about it, and then ask them a question. All of this usually took less than ten minutes. Then the whole family would pray. It worked better when the prayers were specific, so every morning they picked out someone who needed special prayer. This increased his children's sensitivity to the needs of others.

On many mornings Pat's kids' eyes would glaze over, and he'd think, *What am I doing here?* Then one day a woman bumped into his wife. This woman led a discipleship group of high school girls that included his daughter. She said to Patsy, "I don't know what you do in those morning devotions, but it seems that every week something comes up in our group, and your daughter says you just talked about that in your devotions." And the whole time Pat didn't think she had heard a word!

If the thought of doing devotions three or four times a week seems overwhelming, consider a simple starting point. Why not carve out time Sunday after church during lunch, reread the sermon text from that morning, and then discuss how you might apply the pastor's message to your life? You could close with a prayer asking God to use his Word to change your hearts.

The bottom line is this: We believe you cannot be the father God wants you to be unless you regularly lead your family in Bible reading, prayer, and worship.[24]

Neither can you go wrong by encouraging your kids to read the Bible and pray on their own. If we can help them build into their lives the habit of Bible study and prayer, we give them a daily opportunity for God to speak to their hearts—one of the best gifts we could ever give them.

We strongly encourage you to give your kids an incentive to do private devotions. Here's the plan Pat used. Pat told his kids, "If you will do a daily devotion for at least twenty-five days each month, we'll buy you a CD."

"That's nice, Dad," they said.

"That's not all," he added. "In addition, if you do your devotions at least twenty-five days each month for ten out of twelve months, we'll pay you $250. You can miss any two months and still get paid."

Their eyes popped open. "Wow, Dad! Are you kidding?"

"No, we're not kidding. But that's not all. If you will do your devotions all twelve months in row, we'll double the amount and pay you $500. And you still have to do only twenty-five days a month."

They set up an honor system. The kids made up a chart, then marked an X for each day they did a devotion. If they missed a day, they could make it up the next. Does it surprise you to learn that Pat's children consistently did daily devotions all the way through college?

One day, when it came time for the annual renewal of the agreement, the kids conspired against Pat. When he asked them if they wanted to go another year, they said, "Dad, we've been talking, and you don't need to pay us anymore; we're going to be spending time with God anyway." How many children do you know who voluntarily have regular private devotions?

Kids love incentives. You have a big interest in giving your children a heart for God. Why not bring these two interests together? Some may say this amounts to bribing our children to read the Bible, but children do many things for "the wrong reason." Why do young children brush their teeth? Because we make them, not because of concern over good dental hygiene. Why do they do their homework? Out of fear of punishment or loss, not always because they want to learn everything God has for them at school.

Paying your kids to do devotions is no different. The amount of money is unimportant; just make it relevant for your situation. Money serves merely as a tool to help them develop a habit they will have in place when their hearts grow and motivations change.

Help your children do the right thing until their hearts catch up with their habits—but remain focused on the heart. Give your children a daily opportunity to be transformed by the power of God and his Word.

FATHERING THE HEART MEANS DISTINGUISHING BETWEEN IN CHURCH AND IN CHRIST

One problem stands in the way of implementing any of the ideas we've discussed. Our children are great at "playing the game" and learning how to give us what they think we want. Yet, four out of five children who "look good" as Christians drop out of church before they finish high school. Why?

One reason: Even though these children are in church, they are not truly in Christ. *It is not enough for your children to be found in church; they must also be found in Christ.*

Sometimes opportunities to reinforce this truth come at surprising times. When David's daughter, Sarah, was seven, she and her older brother Ryan had an argument and got sent to their rooms. A few minutes later she came out of her room, crying and whining. David's wife, Ruthie, said, "Go back to your room right now."

About five minutes later she came out and said something through her tears that Ruthie couldn't understand, so Ruthie sent her back to her room. This happened several times over the next fifteen minutes. Eventually Sarah went to Ryan's room and asked him her question. Once she got her answer, she calmed down and returned to her room. When Ruthie finally allowed her to come out, she discovered that Sarah had been asking, "Mom, how do you become a Christian?"

Ruthie swallowed the lump in her throat, then reinforced what Ryan had told her about having a relationship with Jesus Christ through faith. Sarah prayed with her mother and asked Jesus to forgive her sins and give her a new heart of love for him. David and Ruthie laughed about it that night—their daughter had been begging unsuccessfully to hear about Jesus and finally had to hear it from her brother!

In reality, all children beg to hear about Jesus, whether they know it or not. Their unfulfilled dreams, dashed hopes, unrelenting frustrations, and hollow victories all cry out for an answer big enough to make sense. The only answer that can satisfy their hearts is Jesus.

The Bible tells us in simple terms what it means to have a relationship with God. Romans 6:23 gives one of the clearest explanations of the gospel: "The wages of sin is death, but the gift of God is eternal life in Christ Jesus our Lord."

This verse tells us that sin—a desire to live independently of God—leads to death. A perfect and holy and just God must remain true to his character and punish sin. When Adam fell into sin, we all fell into sin. So our children are products of both the creation and the Fall. They have great dignity because of their creation in the image of God, but they also are sinners who cannot help but rebel against God's authority.

We have no hope in and of ourselves, so God himself came to rescue us from our sin. The righteous life of Jesus fulfilled the law of God and his death paid the penalty for our sins. His death brings forgiveness from sin and his life becomes our righteousness. So God offers us the free gift of eternal life in Christ Jesus.

Have you accepted this free gift for yourself? This is the first and indispensable step to being able to father your child's heart. God offers you a chance to become a new man in Christ from the inside out. If you have not done so already, why not take time right now and surrender your life to God by asking him to forgive you and give you this new life? Consider praying from your heart, using words something like these:

> *Lord Jesus, I need you in my life. I confess that I have been trying to find happiness in impotent and sinful ways. Thank you for dying on the cross to pay the penalty for my sins. More than any other thing, I know that to be happy I need to put my faith solely in you to be my Savior and Lord. I invite you to take control of my life and show me how to live by faith rather than by trying to be good. Amen.*

If you've just prayed, congratulations and welcome to the family! Why not use this section to explain to your children what it means to follow Jesus, then see if they want to pray the prayer? We want not just children who look good on the outside. We want children who have truly given their hearts to Jesus. Remember, it's not enough for our children to be found in church; they must also be found in Christ.

THE HEART OF THE MATTER

- It's not enough for our children to be found in church; they must also be found in Christ.
- The most important thing we can do for our children is to help them develop a heart for God.
- The first step to fathering our children's hearts is to surrender our own hearts to Christ.
- We can create an environment where our children see the benefits of loving Jesus.
- To help our children develop a heart for God, we should pray for them, teach them, and model our faith before them.
- Fathering the heart means having our children join us in church, involving them in service, and helping them spend time with God.
- Help your children do the right thing until their hearts catch up with their habits.

TAKE IT TO HEART
QUESTIONS FOR APPLICATION AND DISCUSSION

1. Name your number one concern as a father. In what ways has this concern shown itself in the way you father your children?

2. What are you currently doing to give your children a heart for God? Which of the three practical ideas a dad can do— pray, teach, model—most caught your attention, and why? Anything new or different you'd like to try?

3. What are your children currently doing that will give them a heart for God? Which of the three practical ideas your children can do—join you in church, be involved in service, spend time with God—most caught your attention, and why? Anything new or different you'd like to try?

4. Have you surrendered your life to Christ and asked him to forgive your sins? If yes, why not tell your children about your experience? See if they feel ready to become followers of Christ, and lead them through the prayer above. If no, what else would have to happen for you to be willing to give your life to Christ? If you're ready, why not pray the prayer right now?

STRAIGHT TO THE HEART
Applying the Bible to Your Children's Hearts

One of the most important investments we have ever made into the hearts of our children is having regular family devotions.

Set aside ten to fifteen minutes three or four days a week. Some families may want to take a break in the summer when the calendar gets less structured. Don't be legalistic—if your daughter has a "hair crisis," you can skip it that day. Pick a Bible verse that has spoken to you, or find a verse that deals with a topic you want to discuss with your kids (generally or because of a specific circumstance).

Here's one way to go about preparing and delivering a fifteen-minute devotion:

Preparation (15 minutes to 1 hour)

- Ask for a demonstration of the Spirit's power through prayer.

- Pick a Bible verse having to do with a current issue or something that interests you.

- Find the "gravity" in the verse.
  ✓ What problem does it solve?
  ✓ What is the underlying heart issue?
  ✓ What tension needs to be resolved?

- Ask other important questions.
  ✓ What is the writer talking about?
  ✓ What does the writer say?
  ✓ How does the verse help us see more of the greatness of Jesus?

- Remember that asking the right question will produce the right message.

Delivery

- *Arrest their attention* with an interesting question or quote—30 seconds.

- *Set up a problem* that needs to be solved or a question that needs to be answered. Create gravity—one to two minutes.

- *Read your verse and explain . . .*
  ✓ what it says
  ✓ what it means
  ✓ how it addresses the problem or question you have set up

- *State your point in a short, memorable sentence.* What single point do you want them to remember? You might read 2 Corinthians 4:6–18 and say, "When we have an eternal perspective on our troubles, God will help our hearts to not become weary."

- *Illustrate* from your own life, an everyday situation, something you've read, or a famous life. Use quotes and stories. Help them take an unusual look at the usual—to see their situation from a different angle. For example, "When Billy hit you, you joined a long list of other Christians who have been wronged. Someday everything will be made right. In the meantime, God promises to be your friend and to comfort you."

- *Suggest applications.* "When someone acts mean or hurts you with words, you don't have to get even. If someone hurts or tries to hurt you physically, you should tell me about it. For a lot of small hurts, though, you can go directly to Jesus in prayer and ask him to protect and comfort you."

- *Ask for discussion.* Say something like, "How do you think this applies to something you're facing right now?"

- *Ask them how God wants them to respond.* "Based on what God already has done for you through Jesus, what do you think God wants you to think, feel, say, or do differently?"

- *Pray.* Close in prayer (preferably led by one of the children).

When we apply Scripture to the lives of our children, we give them the assurance that there exists a source of truth on which they can rely. They begin to understand that they can trust God's revelation to be their authority. Applying the Bible opens our children's eyes and helps us father their hearts to love God and others.

CHAPTER 9

Disciplining
Your Child's Heart

North Carolina boasts many wonderful views, but perhaps none more beautiful than the hike up Whiteside Mountain. Pat has made the hike a number of times. It's perfect for a family, because everyone can do it without getting too testy. (Okay, Pat's family did get a little testy on the way down when he got them lost, but that's another story.)

Some areas across the top of Whiteside Mountain have railings right up to the edge of steep cliffs. When Pat and his family hiked along those sections, they walked right up to the railings and looked down the cliffs a thousand feet to the canyon below.

As you hike further, the mountaintop opens onto a flat rock that stretches out for a hundred yards or so. It provides a wonderful place to have a picnic. Pat and his family frequently packed lunches for picnics on the big flat rock.

While Pat readily let his two young children walk right up to the edge of a cliff that plunged a thousand feet, he wouldn't let them go within fifty feet of the edge of the big flat rock. The difference? The railings, of course.

Discipline plays the role of railings in our children's lives. Children benefit from discipline. They benefit because discipline lets them know the location of boundaries. Boundaries define not only what is off-limits but also all the places our children can safely go. Discipline keeps our children from wandering into places they should not go, but it also gives them the confidence to explore as far as they should go! Without clear boundaries, our children cannot develop their full potential.

FATHERING THE HEART MEANS HELPING CHILDREN SEE WHAT'S IN THEIR HEARTS

If an outsider watched you discipline your children, would he see anything different from what he might see from a Jewish father? A Muslim father? A moral, agnostic father? If not, you may well be fathering for performance rather than fathering the heart.

The word *discipline* comes from the same root as the word *disciple*, meaning "to train" or "to teach." So discipline becomes an integral tool in the process of discipling the hearts of our children to love God and others.

The goal of discipline is not simply to get our children to obey; if we do that, we merely father for performance. Rather, discipline helps your children see what lies in their hearts so that God can bring them to repentance and faith. That's what fathering the heart is all about.

Often we discipline our children only to get them to do "better." Mike told John, "You need to clean up your room before you can go out tonight." John did clean up his room, but he did it with a bitter attitude. John did "better" but also got "bitter." Nothing had changed in his heart. Getting our children to change their behavior and rise to some acceptable standard is no big deal. We err if we believe that this kind of discipline has accomplished its purpose.

FATHERING THE HEART IS NOT ABOUT ME

Sometimes disciplining children becomes more about us than about our children. Bobby's daughter, Rebecca, came up to him at church while he was talking with some of his friends and asked, "Can I go to the mall this afternoon with Brittany?"

"No," Bobby said, "not on Sundays." Had Rebecca asked him the same question at home, Bobby would have said yes. He only wanted to look like a Sabbath observer to his friends, but his answer didn't come from his heart, and she knew it. She kicked herself for not waiting until later! As a result, an attitude of reverence about Sabbath keeping will not likely make it into Rebecca's heart—at least not by way of her dad.

At other times we just want our kids to stop some annoying behavior. We issue directives more for our convenience than for their good. One day while home alone with his three children, David got busy helping his oldest son with a project. David happened to glance into the kitchen. His three-year-old son was sitting in the middle of the floor—a paper cup by his side—busily unscrewing the cap from a gallon of orange juice. Just beyond him, David's five-year-old daughter was straining on her tiptoes to get an opened bag of pretzels off the shelf.

David quickly played out a scenario of what the next few seconds could bring: Youngest son pours a gallon of orange juice all over the floor. Daughter trips over son and dumps pretzels across the kitchen. Two children stand up, dance, and sing on a kitchen floor covered with orange juice–soaked pretzels. Then David has to clean it all up—and quick!—before his wife comes walking through the door.

So how did the usually calm and mild-mannered David react? He erupted in anger and yelled at his kids. Why did he get angry? David had helped his three-year-old son pour juice dozens of times. David's five-year-old daughter retrieved things out of the pantry every day. Either one of those things, by itself, would not have made him angry. So what seemed different about this episode?

It had become about him, not them. When David saw all those things happening at the same time, he felt a loss of control. He feared he might be inconvenienced by having to clean up a mess.

And getting angry seemed the quickest way for him to regain control and get his own way.

Discipline Is for the Child's Heart

As fathers, we must remember that discipline exists for the child's benefit, not ours. And we also need to remember to discipline with a focus on the heart, not just the behavior.

When we discipline the heart, we hope to create an environment where God can change our children from the inside out. When we talk to our children about their disobedience and sin, our discussion should focus not on *what* they did but rather help them understand *why* they might have done it.

This works well even with young children. Take something as simple as fighting over a toy and hitting another child. The dialogue might go something like this:

Dad: "Eric, why did you hit Kevin?"
Eric: "I didn't hit him that hard."
Dad: "Eric, why did you hit Kevin?"
Eric: "I don't know."
Dad: "I think you do know. Why did you hit Kevin?"
Eric: "He wouldn't let go of my Hot Wheels car."
Dad: "Were you angry when he wouldn't let go of the car?"
Eric: "Kevin is just a crybaby. I hit Tommy twice as hard yesterday, and he hardly cried at all."
Dad: "Eric, were you angry when Kevin wouldn't let go of the car?"
Eric: "Yes."
Dad: "Why do you think that made you angry?"
Eric: "Because I wanted the car."
Dad: "You thought if you had the car you would have more fun?"
Eric: "Yes."

Dad: "Son, you wanted to get your way, and I understand. I feel like that sometimes too. I know it seems as if you will feel happier if you get the toy, but do you know what the Bible says?"

Eric: "What?"

Dad: "The Bible says that in the end we will be happier if we share. God says that if we are selfish, we will be sad, but if we love him and love our friends, we will be happy. Let's pray right now, and I'm going to ask God to help you believe that."

A similar dialogue can take place with a teenager who breaks curfew (he thinks that the fun he can have late at night will bring more joy than honoring his parents), a preteen who continues to hang out with the wrong crowd at school (she believes acceptance from friends will satisfy her heart more than the love of Christ), or a college student who skips classes (she believes doing her own thing will make her happier than being a good steward of the education God is providing). Help your children to understand the lies they are believing and to return to the truth of the gospel.

When you see patterns of sin developing—such as taking advantage of weaker people, intentionally rebelling against authority, manipulating situations to get their way, or habitually lying—as much as possible continue to discipline your children until they have a change of heart, not just a change of behavior. Bring your discipline to bear against the attitude rather than the action.

You can't discipline every sinful act until your child comes to complete repentance. That would drive both of you crazy! But you can prayerfully look for opportunities to help your child deal with what is really going on in their hearts. God can use these times to transform your child's heart.

Be careful not to berate your children about their behavior or attitudes. Once you have clearly pointed out your child's sin and disciplined him, let it go. Leave room for the Holy Spirit to do his work in your child's conscience.

We want our children to enjoy a growing and authentic relationship with Christ, not just learn to please us. While we can never know for sure when our children's attitudes have changed, most fathers know when a child just goes along to get along.

FATHERING THE HEART MEANS NEITHER ALLOWING WHAT GOD PROHIBITS NOR PROHIBITING WHAT GOD ALLOWS

Careful discipline shows how much we love our children. Proverbs 13:24 says, "He who spares the rod hates his son, but he who loves him is careful to discipline him."

It's tough to discipline our children today. Consider the number of debatable issues children face as they grow up. Should they be allowed to read Harry Potter? Should they be allowed to see PG-13 movies, and if so, when? What kind of music should they be allowed to listen to? Should a curfew be 10:00 P.M., 11:00 P.M., or midnight? Does the Bible give fathers any practical wisdom about these things?

We believe it does. *Do not allow what God prohibits, and do not prohibit what God allows.*

We will go out on a limb and say that this is the most helpful idea for discipline you will ever read. To allow what God prohibits is what theologians call "license," an inappropriate sense of freedom to disobey God's clear commands. To prohibit what God allows is called "legalism," an inappropriate reliance on following rules to be considered righteous before God. Either one will poison your relationship with your children.

Error #1: Allowing What God Prohibits

Juan's mom and dad both work. Juan's dad travels just about every week.

Starting when he was ten, Juan got in the habit of riding around the neighborhood every day after school, playing with other kids until his mother got home from work. Four years later, what used to be innocent wandering has become a search for mischief—smoking, graffiti, and vandalism of public areas. Police recently arrested Juan for threatening another child in the presence of an adult.

A few Christian families have taken an interest in Juan, but surrogate parents find it tough to provide the structure he needs. Juan's mom has basically given up and allows him to have his own way. His dad gets mad when something big happens but otherwise doesn't much care. So Juan just does whatever he wants—and he wants to do more and more of what God prohibits. No one in his life has shown a willingness to drive the folly from his heart. No one has said, "Yes, I love you, but no, you can't have your own way."

We often allow what God prohibits when we provide too little structure for our kids. Children need clear boundaries, but they also need to "buy in." Many parents accomplish this buy-in with periodic family meetings. David and Ruthie regularly get their children together to talk about important family issues. They give airtime to all three of their children to raise any concerns they have, and they make sure that everyone has a chance to express their feelings about each issue. Last month, their nine-year-old daughter said, "I don't like it when the boys poke me or push me for no reason." (Apparently, her brothers have a habit of shoving or punching her when they walk by. Of course, when one of the boys does it to the other, they call it affection!)

Ruthie, an only girl in her own family, could sympathize. The family talked about this issue and how it made each person feel. Together they judged it to be inappropriate behavior. Then they established the consequences if it were to happen again. David ended the meeting with a prayer, asking God to help them love one another from the heart and to demonstrate this love in their actions.

FATHERING THE HEART MEANS
REQUIRING FIRST-TIME OBEDIENCE

Once we have agreement on an issue, we need to require first-time obedience from our children. This solves so many problems. It helps the child develop an attitude of appropriate respect and submission to parents. It helps you as a father because it short-circuits the power struggles that often lead to frustration and anger. And it also helps little problems from "growing up" into big ones.

Willie Richardson, a pastor-friend of ours, told how a member of his church came to him with a problem. As he listened he saw that it was a tremendous mess involving a number of broken relationships. It all began with a misunderstanding between two people. He told the church member, "Why didn't you bring this problem to me right away while it was still a cute, little cuddly problem you could hold in the palm of your hand? Instead, you tried to solve it yourself, and now it is an eight-foot-tall monster devouring everything in its path."

That's how it is with discipline. If you require first-time obedience from your children, then defiance gets exposed while it remains "a cute, little cuddly problem." If you don't require first-time obedience, you will soon be looking at an "eight-foot-tall monster."

When your children don't obey the first time, you need to apply consequences. We believe the Bible allows for discretion in disciplining your children. Spanking, time-outs, loss of privileges, or other natural consequences all may be appropriate. Whichever method you choose, make sure your child understands you are disciplining their attitudes and not just their actions.

Error #2: Prohibiting What God Allows

Decisions. Many choices our children make are not moral choices between right and wrong, but priority choices between right and right. There may be no one "right" answer—although you may recognize one as wiser than another. Suppose Alexa has to decide whether to take regular or advanced algebra next year. Kendrick feels torn between playing soccer or baseball. Elizabeth wants to buy a game for the computer but such a choice will use up almost all of her spending money.

Our children need the freedom to make some of these decisions on their own, even if they don't make the wisest choices (or the ones we would have made). We have to give our kids a little wiggle room! If we provide too much structure for them, we can actually prohibit what God allows.

Expectations. Those who father for performance give their kids the impression that they have to be perfect or live up to impossibly high expectations. This creates incredible pressure and can lead to our children to feel a false sense of shame. We can cause this problem by asking our children to reason "beyond their years" (see "Straight to the Heart," page 27). Look for ways to send your children the powerful message, "You don't have to be perfect for me."

Dreams. We create shame when we shoot down our children's ideas and dreams because they seem impractical or inefficient. Tom's twelve-year-old daughter said, "Hey, Dad, when I grow up I want to be a fireman like you." Tom replied, "Janie, you'll never be a fireman. You need to think about what it is that girls do when they grow up." Why prohibit what God allows? Wouldn't it be better to encourage rather than shame a child's dreams?

Your child's lemonade stand won't likely make her the next Bill Gates, but you need to let her find out for herself. Your son's band probably won't become the next U2, but maybe you should allow him to pursue his dream as far as his interest and talent take him.

When we father like this, we provide railings for our children's hearts—railings that create freedom within boundaries. Because they know the outside limits, they also feel great freedom to explore the rest of the rock.

Positive Reinforcement. When we focus on positive reinforcement, we find a great way to guard against prohibiting what God allows. Rafael hates his job because his boss talks to him only when he has done something wrong. Jim's marriage suffers partly because his wife constantly emphasizes his mistakes. Does anyone like hanging around someone who habitually points out his or her flaws? Our children feel the same way.

We must consciously balance correction, punishment, and teaching on the one hand and positive reinforcement on the other. When we discipline a child for a particular attitude or action and the child shows improvement, it is important to say, "You know, son, the last time you ate cookies before dinner and we asked you about it, you lied. Even though you've eaten cookies again before dinner, I want you to know I appreciate you telling the truth." Think about what that sets up in the child's mind: *When I make mistakes, I don't have to keep secrets.* That's fathering the heart.

FATHERING THE HEART MEANS BALANCING STRUCTURE AND FREEDOM

We dads tend to provide too much structure where we should allow freedom, and allow too much freedom where we should provide structure.

Consider the tendency to provide too much structure where we ought to allow freedom. Too often we father for performance by dictating minor aspects of our children's behavior. When Pat's son, John, was in tenth grade, he decided he wanted to bleach his hair. Pat and Patsy talked it over and decided to let him experiment with things that would not involve permanent changes, such as tattoos and body piercings. Today John is a married man with his natural hair color, and everyone's happy.

At other times, we give too much freedom where we should provide structure. When Sandra went in her room and closed the door, she tuned her radio to the hip-hop station. She knew some of the lyrics were inappropriate, but so long as she listened through earphones, she figured her parents would never know.

Reggie sat at the back of the class with Kendrick, the class clown. Kendrick got them in trouble sometimes, but Reggie's grades remained good, and that's all his parents seemed to care about.

Too often our attitude becomes "out of sight, out of mind." Yet, these everyday moments express the hopes, dreams, and fears of our children. They represent crucially important times for us to provide structure to help shape the worldview and attitudes of our child's heart.

FATHERING THE HEART MEANS TRANSFERRING RESPONSIBILITY

All fathers who want to discipline their child's heart face the challenge of watching the focus boomerang back on them for what they are doing or not doing. If you have teenagers, you may experience this every day. "You won't let me go to my friend's house, you won't let me do a sleepover, you're making me do my chores so I can't be with my friends." Instead of getting caught up in the blame game, transfer as much responsibility as appropriate from you to the child.

Most teenage boys do not rise early, and Pat's son was no exception. He developed a habit of sleeping in that put the whole family behind in the morning. He also began getting tardy slips at school. So Pat and Patsy found themselves in a power struggle. One morning, Pat briefly considered going in his boy's room to drag him out. Instead, they decided to transfer the responsibility for this choice to their son. They worked it out with the school that if he received six tardy slips, he would have to stay after school for two hours, clean up trash, and help around the grounds.

"We are not going to argue with you anymore about getting out of bed," Pat said to his son, "but if you get up late, we're also not going to rush to get you to school on time. If you're late, you're late. It's your choice. And you know the consequences."

Guess how many tardy slips Pat's son had at the end of the semester? That's right, five. He never seemed to get that sixth one. Somehow he found the strength to get out of bed every morning because his parents transferred the responsibility to him.

FATHERING THE HEART MEANS
HEARING THE BEST TESTIMONY OF ALL

Many philosophies of discipline exist in the world today. One biblical philosophy of discipline centers on the gospel. Within this biblical philosophy of discipline, a father has a wide range of things he can do. It gives a lot of freedom about the particulars. But one thing remains clear: Biblical discipline focuses on the attitudes and beliefs of our children's hearts, not their behavior.

No doubt you've heard someone tell one of those gripping, goose bumps–inducing stories of how God changed his life. It may even be your own story. We love to hear about men who were ensnared by violence, crime, drugs, alcohol, and abuse of all kinds, and then hear how God miraculously changed them. It thrills us to hear how God changes lives.

If you study such a man's history, you probably will find a father who failed him. Maybe his dad wasn't around much. Maybe he provided too much structure. Maybe he let his son run wild. Maybe he just didn't care. Whatever the case, this man's father didn't drive the folly out of his boy's heart.

But remember, for a man to stand in front of an audience with a testimony like that, a lot of people had to pay a very steep price. A mother who soaked her pillow in tears. A father who practically lived at the doctor's office because his headaches wouldn't allow him to get any sleep. A wife who woke up in the morning and couldn't get out of bed because she didn't know how she could make it through another day. A little girl who prayed, "God, please help my daddy to stop hitting me."

How much better the testimony that says, "My dad loved me, and I couldn't have my own way. My father disciplined me, and I respect him. He loved me enough to provide structure, but he also cared enough to make sure I had healthy freedom. I grew into a person who loves God and others from the heart because of my dad."

If your children can someday give a testimony like this, just think how happy you, your wife, *and* your children will be!

THE HEART OF THE MATTER

- Discipline helps our children to see what lies in their hearts so God can bring them to repentance and faith.
- Too often we discipline more for our convenience than for our children's good.
- Discipline should help our children to understand the lies they believe and then to return to the gospel.
- Do not allow what God prohibits, and do not prohibit what God allows.
- Fathering the heart means providing structure and requiring first-time obedience.
- Fathering the heart means neither forcing our children to live up to unrealistic expectations nor crushing their dreams.
- We tend to provide too much structure where we should allow freedom and allow too much freedom where we should provide structure.
- Fathering the heart means transferring responsibility to our children.

TAKE IT TO HEART
QUESTIONS FOR APPLICATION AND DISCUSSION

1. What do the following verses say about the importance of disciplining our children?
   - Proverbs 13:24 _____
   - Proverbs 22:15 _____
   - Hebrews 12:5–11 _____

2. Which idea in this chapter most resonated with you, and why?

3. Have you ever provided too much structure where there should be freedom? If so, in what ways? Have you ever given too much freedom where your children need more structure? If so, in what ways? How can you get involved in their lives to help provide structure in critical areas?

4. Think about your interactions with your children over the last two weeks. Ask them the following questions and get their honest feedback:
   - "Do you feel like I put too much pressure on you?"
   - "Do you ever feel like I prohibit things that God allows?"
   - "Do you ever feel like I allow things that God prohibits?"
   - "Do you know that I love you no matter what you do?"
   - "Do I give you enough positive reinforcement?"
   - "Do you feel like I provide a good balance of structure and freedom?"

STRAIGHT TO THE HEART
Dealing with Foul Language

Almost all fathers, at one time or another, have to work with their children about foul language. Children inevitably push the envelope with cursing, many times in a way almost deliberately designed to provoke their parents. How should we handle it when our children use foul language?

First, we need to understand why this kind of talk is inappropriate. The issue is *not* that there is a list of English words that the Bible says is off-limits and should never be spoken. Many times we discipline our children as though these syllables and sound waves were somehow unholy and sinful in and of themselves. Of course, this isn't the case.

Most curse words function simply as synonyms for other words that seem more acceptable, and in many cases there exist appropriate ways to use these "curse" words in real sentences (as in the case of "hell," "damn," and "Jesus").

So if the sounds and words themselves don't make language inappropriate, what does? And how should we discipline our children?

God disapproves of foul language because of what it reveals about our children's hearts. Human beings curse for a variety of sinful reasons: anger at circumstances and, by extension, God; trying to impress or shock others; laziness; or not loving and respecting those who may find offense in our words. The real issue comes down to what is going on in the minds and hearts of our children when they curse.

So Paul writes, "Do not let any unwholesome talk come out of your mouths, but only what is helpful for building others up" (Ephesians 4:29). When our children gain a heart of love for others before themselves, they will take care to say helpful and profitable things. When they focus on themselves and fixate on their own desires and needs, they will say unwholesome and unhelpful things.

Help your children to understand that what they say represents something going on in their hearts. They have believed a selfish lie, and they need to turn from this to trust Christ alone. Help them understand that their words can bless people made in God's image (James 3:9). When they love God and others, their speech will reflect this love in their hearts.

Here's one way this could work:

Suppose that you and your son are walking to the car after a close basketball game, surrounded by other parents and their sons and children. Your son yells in anger, "I can't believe how bad we got screwed by the ref!"

You could calmly take him aside privately and say, "I know you feel upset. I'm sure it seemed like all the calls went against you. Still, that kind of language isn't appropriate. To some people, screw means 'to treat unfairly,' but to others it's a term for sexual activity, and that offends them. God wants us to show respect for others by using language that doesn't needlessly offend them."

This dad understands that the words his son uses reflect what is happening in his heart.

CHAPTER 10

Sexuality: The Birds and the Bees

Ellen and Anna grew up down the street from one another.

When Ellen was eight, she convinced her mother to buy her a skimpy, two-piece bathing suit, just like the one Jenny, her favorite baby-sitter, wore. Her mom and dad said, "It's no big deal. She's only a little girl."

When Anna was eight, her dad led their family in devotions once a week. They talked about how Jesus can change their lives. Over time, they discussed the characteristics of a godly woman, including modesty.

When Ellen was eleven, she began changing from a girl to a woman. She looked through the magazines her mother brought home from the grocery store to see what kind of woman she wanted to become.

When Anna was eleven, her dad took her out to celebrate her birthday. They had a nice dinner together and finished with some ice cream at the mall.

When Ellen was thirteen, she kissed a boy for the first time. He was fifteen and told her that he thought she was really hot.

When Anna was thirteen, her dad gave her a promise ring. He told her that she was very special and that she should wait until marriage to give her heart to a man.

When Ellen was fifteen, her mom and dad got on her case about her clothes and hair. The clever Ellen soon discovered a great system—she just took off her bra and changed tops after she left the house.

When Anna was fifteen, she went to the store with her friend Katie. They saw the season's new clothes, but neither one wanted to try them on. They didn't want to demean themselves by wearing something so provocative.

When Ellen was seventeen, she had sex with a college freshman. Her parents allowed her to visit him one weekend on campus, and she decided the time was right. It wasn't all it was cracked up to be.

When Anna was seventeen, she went on a mission trip with her church youth group. Her boyfriend, Chad, joined her on the trip, so she asked a college-age counselor to help her stay accountable.

When Ellen was nineteen, she got pregnant for the second time. Since the man she lived with had turned out to be a jerk, she decided she wouldn't have this baby either.

When Anna was nineteen, she met Doug, a funny and handsome young man who was committed to Christ. He told her that he valued their relationship too much to mess it up by getting involved sexually before marriage.

When Ellen was twenty-two, she wept as she pulled into her parents' driveway. Little Ricky screamed in his car seat. Even though Rick had left her two days before, it still had taken a while for her to work up the courage to call and see if she could come home to her mom and dad. She had nowhere else to turn. After getting Ricky out of the car, she walked slowly to the front door, wishing she could start her life over again.

When Anna was twenty-two, she and Doug hailed a taxi to bring them home from the airport after their honeymoon. Doug carried her over the threshold of their apartment. When he set her down, she looked him in the eyes and knew it had all been worth it. What a fantastic way to start a life together!

FATHERING THE HEART MEANS
HELPING YOUR CHILDREN UNDERSTAND SEX

Will your child's story more closely resemble Ellen's or Anna's? We work with many men who reared "Ellens," both girls and boys who shipwrecked their lives because of sex. And we've seen a few "Annas," young women and men whose fathers helped them treat sex with the honor and respect it deserves.

There may be no area of life with the potential to bring as much pleasure or destruction as sex. God has given it to us as a gift, but the Fall has corrupted and perverted it.

All children today get steamrolled by a blitzkrieg of sinful sexual cues, from commercials to billboards to movies to magazines at the checkout line. As one Christian counselor said, "The entertainment industry and media are sexually abusing our children." Someone else said, "Sex has been reduced to plumbing." The result? Many of today's young people end up with trampled, crushed hearts because of a distorted view of sex.

How can we prepare our children for this bombardment? How do we give them the tools they need to gain a healthy view of sex in this fallen world? Before we look at what the Bible says about God's design for sex, we need to understand our current situation. Too many Christians feel frustrated and confused because they have unknowingly adopted a view of sexuality shaped more by the culture than by the Bible.

The "Sex Is Dirty" (Victorian) View

Jason's mom and dad never said much about sex, other than that you shouldn't talk about it. His "private parts" (they never used the real words) were dirty. He hated changing clothes at the YMCA or in a locker room, because he felt ashamed to have anyone else see his body.

By the time Jason reached the fifth grade, he knew where babies came from, but not because his mom and dad told him. He heard it from his friends at school, who also told him about condoms and "the bases" (first base is kissing; second, breasts; third, genitals; and fourth, intercourse). Sex seemed scary and mysterious and somehow a little wrong. But Jason could also tell it must be a lot of fun.

Jason's family had a Victorian view of sex, not a biblical one. In this view, sex is a private thing that should never be discussed. Our bodies have parts that are embarrassing at best and dirty at worst. For people who have this mind-set, sex is a necessary evil. Or, if they enjoy sex, they feel ashamed that it seems fun.

When this view combines with the sexual and psychological abuse that so many young people—especially women—suffer, you have a recipe for disaster. Sex gets viewed as a filthy, shameful activity. Some married people, particularly women, see sex as an obligation, so they "give in" occasionally for the sake of their spouses.

Ironically, most "traditional" Americans hold a very Victorian viewpoint. For all practical purposes, this view denies that God instituted sex as a holy activity. Children immersed in this view grow up confused and fearful. They carry huge baggage into marriage. They feel embarrassed to get naked or to see their spouse naked. They always feel guilt and inhibition about being intimate. Often it takes years of frustration, bitterness, and disappointment before they can reestablish a healthy view of sex.

The "Sex Is Natural" (Hedonistic) View

Theresa knew her mom and dad had lived together before they got married. She'd also read some of her mom's romance novels and seen the *Joy of Sex* book on her dad's bookshelf. By the time she became a senior in high school, she decided she wanted to try it out for herself.

During the sexual revolution of the 1960s, young people cast the old morality overboard to search for experience and pleasure—and sex. For a lot of people, sex amounts to just one more activity that brings pleasure, with little or no meaning beyond its physical sensations. A young woman said, "I don't feel guilty about having sex because it's the natural thing to do." This sentiment carries enough truth to justify a good lie.

Our secular culture promotes this view in thousands of ways. Many hit movies champion the view by sympathetically showing unmarried couples who get involved sexually. Magazines and television speak of sex as a recreational activity. Our kids get this message loud and clear. A recent study of seventeen hundred sixth through ninth graders showed that over half believed a couple should have sex if they have been dating for more than six months.[25]

When our children absorb either of these two faulty views, it inevitably leads to frustration. They may get a sense that "something better is out there," but they can't identify what it is unless we tell them. Better they get it right the first time around.

FATHERING THE HEART MEANS TEACHING GOD'S DESIGN FOR SEX

The apostle Paul shows us God's design for sex: "'For this reason a man will leave his father and mother and be united to his wife, and the two will become one flesh.' This is a profound mystery—but I am talking about Christ and the church" (Ephesians 5:31–32).

This passage reveals three important truths we need to teach our children.

1. Human Sexuality Is a Good Gift from God

God brought man and woman together and told them to become "one flesh." The intimacy of "one flesh" obviously involves more than just sex but certainly not less. Our children need to understand that God ordained sex as the highest expression of physical intimacy between a husband and a wife.

In Genesis 2:25, we see that the man and woman were "both naked, and they felt no shame." God intended for men and women to celebrate their spiritual and emotional intimacy through the free and open expression of physical intimacy. This is why sex can bring such great joy.

Don't allow your children to get trapped in a view that sees sex as a duty or obligation. The Bible clearly contradicts the Victorian mind-set that sex is shameful or dirty. The Bible tells us that sex should bring joy and satisfaction: "May your fountain be blessed, and may you rejoice in the wife of your youth. A loving doe, a graceful deer—may her breasts satisfy you always, may you ever be captivated by her love" (Proverbs 5:18–19).

That doesn't sound very Victorian to us! On the other hand, the Bible clearly contradicts the hedonistic perspective that views sex as a natural instinct and therefore okay in any context. God doesn't put any limits on sex; he puts limits on sexual immorality:

> The body is not meant for sexual immorality, but for the Lord, and the Lord for the body. . . .
>
> Flee from sexual immorality. All other sins a man commits are outside his body, but he who sins sexually sins against his own body. Do you not know that your body is a temple of the Holy Spirit, who is in you, whom you have received from God? You are not your own; you were bought at a price. Therefore honor God with your body.
>
> 1 Corinthians 6:13, 18–20

Many issues can contribute to a warped perspective of sex: sexual abuse, lack of information, insensitivity of a spouse, health issues, stress, or lack of faith. Whatever the source, someone who sees sex as drudgery will miss out on a great blessing and can ask Christ by faith for healing.[26]

2. Sex Is Holy Because It Mirrors the Closeness of Our Relationship with Christ

The hedonistic view of sexuality so prevalent today sees sex as a fun, natural activity, just like any other. Eat ice cream, watch a sunset, read a good book, enjoy a round of golf, have sex—they're all the same.

Yet the Bible insists there is so much more to intimacy in marriage than just physical pleasure. It may sound weird if you've never thought about it, but Paul teaches that the oneness we experience in marriage points to the oneness between Christ and the church:

> He who loves his wife loves himself. After all, no one ever hated his own body, but he feeds and cares for it, just as Christ does the church—for we are members of his body. "For this reason a man will leave his father and mother and be united to his wife, and the two will become one flesh." This is a profound mystery—but I am talking about Christ and the church.
>
> Ephesians 5:28–32

Paul teaches that marriage provides "a picture" or "a sample" of the intimacy and closeness between Christ and his bride, the church. Then he quotes Moses (from Genesis 2:24) about what happens when a man and woman marry. Marriage unites two distinct people into a mysterious, spiritual union the Bible calls "one flesh." Lastly, Paul puts the analogy of marriage into the category of a "mystery." And not just any kind of mystery, but a "profound" mystery. What does Paul mean—what's so mysterious? By its nature, a "mystery" is something that escapes full explanation. Here's what we do know: Paul says the mystery involves how closely the marriage union resembles the union Christ has with his church. Sure, marriage is but a shadow, a pointer, but it still provides a true foretaste of the spiritual union we have with Christ.

Marriage gives us the closest example on earth to what we will experience in heaven. To become "one flesh" with a woman will get you the closest to heaven you will ever experience on earth. That's why it stinks to see popular culture reduce marriage and true intimacy to a disposable relationship.

We need to grasp this truth for our own marriages and instill it in our children. Why do we need to teach our children to respect sex? Because marriage offers the highest form of human intimacy. And sex—with its vulnerability, acceptance, emotional connection, and oneness—forms such a sacred part of this intimacy.

Sex is more than just fun. God intends that the intimacy of a man and a woman point us to the closeness we have with Jesus. In the same way that seeing a million stars reveals God's power, the oneness we experience in marriage points us to the spiritual reality of our relationship with Christ.

One young person who heard that sex outside of marriage is wrong said, "I am not challenging you but am merely curious. Where in the Bible does it say God forbids sex before marriage? I have always wondered about that one."

Your kids will ask this question. Why does sex outside of marriage so offend God? Is it simply a bad idea? Paul says, "Do you not know that your bodies are members of Christ himself? Shall I then take the members of Christ and unite them with a prostitute? Never!" (1 Corinthians 6:15). God condemns sex outside of marriage because our bodies belong to Christ. So sex outside of marriage always destroys, regardless of any momentary thrill. Teach your children that God designed sex so a married couple could enjoy intimacy as a reminder of their intimacy with him.

The Bible needs to say something only once for it to have moral authority; repetition merely adds weight. Consider a few of the best (there are more) texts on the subject: Matthew 15:19–20; Acts 15:20, 28–29; 1 Corinthians 5:1–5, 9–11; 6:13–20; 10:8; Galatians 5:19–25; Ephesians 5:3–8; Colossians 3:5; 1 Thessalonians 4:3–8; Jude 7.

3. Sex Reflects Something of What It Means to Be Made in the Image of God

At the end of each of the first five days of creation, God called his work "good." After the creation of man on the sixth day, God called it "very good." So it startles us to read in Genesis 2:18 that he calls something "not good." God declared it "not good" for man to be alone.

God made us for relationships. The creation story shows that intimacy with others is essential to our humanness. Sex represents the highest form of physical intimacy between two people—which explains why even hedonists consider adultery such a betrayal. Somehow, sex taps into the very heart of our personhood. So Paul can say that "all other sins a man commits are outside his body, but he who sins sexually sins against his own body" (1 Corinthians 6:18).

To nick the corner of the Mona Lisa would be unfortunate; to spill paint on her face would be tragic. Paul says that sexual promiscuity wrecks the whole gallery.

FATHERING THE HEART MEANS COMMUNICATING WITH YOUR CHILDREN ABOUT SEX

"Son," a dad said, "I think it's time we had a talk about sex."

"Sure, Dad," the boy replied. "What do you want to know?"

In real life, Pat discovered that teenage boys really don't know much about sex. Pat met with a group of young men recently, and one asked, "What things should someone my age know about sex?" Another wanted to know, "If sex is so good, why should we have to wait?"

Children are naturally curious about sex. They will learn everything they need to know about sex from somewhere. Would you rather it be from their friends, Tom Cruise, a porn star, or you?

We don't have any choice as fathers. Even though sexual discussions can be embarrassing and delicate, sex is too powerful and too dangerous to neglect to deal with head-on. Thirty years ago a girl who had sex could get pregnant; today, in the age of AIDS, she could die. Not including AIDS victims, 56 million adults have an incurable sexually transmitted disease.

What should you communicate to your children about sex, and how?

Clearly explain God's design for sex. Use the Scriptures mentioned above to help your children understand the holiness and sanctity of sex within marriage. As the issue of sex gets raised by life situations, take the opportunity to give your children a biblical view of sexuality.

Tell your children, for example, "A fire is a wonderful thing in a fireplace, but it can also burn your house down. The same thing is true of sex. Married couples have become one person in God's sight, and sex between them expresses this unity. Sex is holy and good, but it can burn you if you don't use it the way God intended."

In an age-appropriate way, clearly explain the biological details about sexuality. Use appropriate biological names for body parts, like penis and vagina. Be matter-of-fact, and handle these terms as you would do with any other aspect of our bodies. Answer your kids' questions about where babies come from.[27]

Model healthy attitudes toward sex and your body. Show appropriate affection and tenderness to your spouse in front of your children. Don't feel embarrassed about your body or your children's bodies.

Jamal's eleven-year-old son, Tony, called him into his room at night. Tony pointed to his groin area. "Dad, should I feel a raised line on my ball down here?"

"Do you mean a bump or raised line on your testicle?" Jamal asked. When Jamal used the word "testicle," his son looked embarrassed. "It's probably normal—there are lots of veins that carry blood to your testicle and penis, but if it changes or gets sore, be sure to let me know. And I'll be glad to look at it for you also." Tony quickly declined his dad's offer, but Jamal took the opportunity to show Tony that he didn't need to feel embarrassed by his body.

Help your children set appropriate boundaries and protect themselves. You and your children can agree on lots of simple boundaries. Tell your teenagers, "Because sexual temptation is so strong, even though you may have good intentions, you should never be alone with someone of the opposite sex in their home or our home or anywhere behind closed doors. Don't ever lie down with someone or caress them in any area of their body that a soccer uniform would normally cover. Also, you should not talk in a way to arouse them sexually. You should not rub your bodies together, even with your clothes on. Once you start experimenting, it is very hard to turn back."

Answer their questions about sex, even the ones they don't ask. Your children will hear contradictory information about sex from a variety of sources. They need help sorting it all out. Below we suggest "the list" for the major talks you will want to have.

You can provide helpful guidance on the difficult area of masturbation. Masturbation becomes a big issue for many teenagers, especially boys. We recognize this as a controversial issue and a matter of conscience. But we also know that studies have shown almost all teenage boys engage in such behavior.

The Bible does not directly address masturbation, though it easily could have.[28] The Scriptures do call lust a sin, and feeding lust leads to sinful behavior. We would suggest, as Dr. James Dobson does,[29] that you discuss masturbation as part of "the talk" as you prepare your son for adolescence.

In the same conversation, warn your children about the dangers of obsessively thinking about sex, getting involved with pornography, or dwelling on sexual fantasies. Discuss God's view of sexuality and the importance of purity. Answer other questions they may have, such as helping them understand why oral sex is still sex in God's eyes.

After this conversation, continue to maintain open lines of natural, comfortable communication about sexuality. Let's say you and your children see a particularly sensual commercial on TV. This would be a good time to say something like this: "It's amazing how obsessed our culture is with sex. It makes it hard to keep our heads straight, but it's important we don't start thinking like many others think. A lot of people have made their lives miserable by acting out what that commercial showed. God gave sex for couples to enjoy in marriage, and that's the only place it will ultimately bring happiness."

Without invading your children's privacy, get involved in their relationships and make it clear that you remain available to discuss anything they would like to discuss.

"The List"

For your convenience, here's a summary list of the topics your discussion should cover at appropriate ages:

ages five to eleven:

- where babies come from and how they are made
- your body—its parts and their function
- God's plan for sex—making babies and pleasure for married couples

age twelve on:

- the sanctity and dignity of sex; moral and spiritual considerations
- lust
- boundaries, guarding the heart, safeguards
- dating and sex[30]
- premarital sex
- sexually transmitted diseases
- masturbation
- pornography, sexual fantasies, *Sports Illustrated* swimsuit edition
- how far is too far: touching, rubbing
- oral sex
- homosexuality
- forgiveness for sexual sin

FATHERING THE HEART MEANS CULTIVATING A CLOSE RELATIONSHIP WITH YOUR DAUGHTER

If you have a son, he will probably need a lot of information from you as he enters adolescence. Your role as the father of a daughter may be even more important as she becomes a young woman.

While most men feel a great need to do something significant with their lives, most women feel a great need for intimacy. An intimate couple can say to each other, "I know who you are at the very deepest level, and I accept you as you are." Your daughter will long to hear this from a man.

The more familial intimacy and closeness between you and your daughter, the less likely she will look for this in the arms of a young man. Take her on dates and demonstrate how a man should treat a woman. Don't be afraid to touch her in appropriate ways—give her a hug, pat her shoulders, or sit beside her on the sofa. Don't make the mistake of pulling back from your daughter at the time she needs you most. Many men stop hugging their daughters when they begin to develop breasts—at the very moment they need Dad's attention more than ever.

What your children think about sex will have a tremendous impact on their lives. It can bring great joy; it can also bring almost endless heartache. What a wonderful opportunity to father the heart and help them celebrate everything God has for them!

THE HEART OF THE MATTER

- Many Christians have a "sex is dirty" (Victorian) view of sex.
- Our culture often teaches our kids to see sex as simply another fun activity.
- Children need to view sex as a good gift from God.
- Sexual intimacy pictures the closeness Christians have with Jesus.
- Sex touches something at the very core of our beings.
- As fathers we don't have any choice: to father our child's heart we must clearly communicate with them about sex.
- Fathering your daughter's heart means continuing to cultivate a close relationship as she grows and develops.

TAKE IT TO HEART
QUESTIONS FOR APPLICATION AND DISCUSSION

1. How did you learn about sex? Did your father help you understand the changes you were going through and what you could expect? What impact did this have on you?

2. Did you grow up with a "sex is dirty" Victorian, "sex is natural" hedonistic, or a biblical view of sex? How has your experience affected you? How does it affect the way you parent? What changes, if any, would you like to make?

3. Have you had "the talk" about sex in an age-appropriate way with each of your children? Why or why not?

4. How can "The List" help you make sure your children learn God's view of sex from you?

STRAIGHT TO THE HEART
Fathering the Heart of a Wayward Child

Even if you do your best as a father, you have no guarantee that your children will always love God and others. Some children will make choices to run from God, and we will feel powerless to stop it. Perhaps nothing seems more agonizing to a father than this.

Jack Miller, a pastor and seminary teacher, felt shock when his eighteen-year-old daughter, Barbara, in a rage one day announced that she wasn't a Christian. Frankly, he and his wife, Rose Marie, had no idea how to handle it. Over the next few years, God taught them some tremendous lessons. God used their enduring love and the love of other Christians to draw Barbara back to himself.

Consider a few principles they learned:[31]

Don't expect more than your child has to give. When Barbara first told her parents that she wasn't a Christian, they did not want to accept it. Gradually, though, they realized that in order to love Barbara, they had to see her for who she really was. This meant giving up a desire to have her behave like a Christian. They could no longer control her choices or express their displeasure at her poor decisions. She was only living out the sinful desires that filled her heart.

Focus on the conscience and the heart, not the behavior. Once the Millers dealt with Barbara's denial of Christ, they set out to build a friendship with her based on truth and love. They stuck to their own convictions, such as not allowing her to sleep with her live-in boyfriend in their house, but at the same time they had them over for dinner and built a relationship with him.

Ask God to help you forgive your child from your heart. To love a wayward child, you must consistently allow Christ to take away negative attitudes toward him or her. Even if you have been hurt many times, you can't suppress these negative experiences and expect to overcome them yourself. God has to change your heart:

> Crippled parents—those who have never had the basements of their lives thoroughly cleaned—will inevitably interfere with Christ's work in the child's life. Christ wants to reach the young person, to find that lost child, for he loves that wandering spirit. But the Spirit's convicting work will be severely hindered by a parent's unconscious rejection. . . . Parents therefore must cultivate their relationships with their own heavenly Father, because only from him can parents learn to forgive, bless, and love.[32]

Enduring love is God's weapon of choice to defeat a rebellious heart. God has shown his enduring love to each of us. He has pursued us with patience and accepted us back with joy. He asks us to be his instruments with our children. Look for opportunities to love and serve your children. Welcome their friends into your family, no matter what kind of people they are. Serve them when they get sick, rejoice with them when they feel well. Help them find jobs, baby-sit their children—do whatever it takes.

Pray in faith that God will lead your child to repentance. For many years, Jack and Rose Marie followed their public love for Barbara with intense private prayer. They believed that God could and would use circumstances to draw Barbara back to himself. For a long time they saw no evidence that this was happening, as Barbara moved further and further away from both her family and Christ. Eventually, however, Christ began to change her heart. After seven years of rebellion, Barbara and her husband asked Christ to forgive their sins and give them new life.

Having a wayward child places a tremendous burden on your shoulders, but it also gives you a tremendous opportunity. See it as an opportunity to experience the riches of God's grace in your own life, and then to see him work in the life of another. We pray that God would use your enduring love to help bring your child back to him.

CHAPTER 11

A Child
Who Loves People

Babies are cute, cuddly, and adorable. A giggle or smile can melt the hardest heart. Of course, we know this is not the whole story.

Many years ago the Minnesota Crime Commission published an intriguing conclusion:

> Every baby starts life as a little savage. He is completely selfish and self-centered. He wants what he wants when he wants it: his bottle, his mother's attention, his playmate's toy, his uncle's watch. Deny him these once, and he seethes with rage and aggressiveness, which would be murderous were he not so helpless. He is, in fact, dirty. He has no morals, no knowledge, no skills. This means that all children—not just certain children—are born delinquent. If permitted to continue in the self-centered world of his infancy, given free reign to his impulsive actions to satisfy his wants, every child would grow up a criminal: a thief, a killer, or a rapist.[33]

David helped lead a campus ministry when he attended Furman University. Jeff, the lead staff member from another university, came to meet with the leaders at Furman once or twice a year. David still remembers how much everyone looked forward to these visits. Jeff had a way of making people feel special. He made it clear that he took an interest in you as a person. He looked you in the eye; he listened; he did the little things that made you feel like the most important person in the world. He seemed to exude the love of Christ.

Jeff could relate to anyone. He felt as comfortable with party boys from the fraternity as he did with devout leaders of the campus ministry. He interacted with professors and members of the maintenance staff. Jeff made an impression on everyone he met. His great secret? He loved people and showed more interest in them than in himself.

How can we fathers take a child like the one described in the Minnesota Crime Commission study and mold him or her into a loving, Christlike human being like Jeff?

Fathering the Heart Means Reproducing Who We Are

Recently Pat had what one might call a technological bad-hair day. He woke up on a Tuesday morning and wanted to get an early start. He works from a home office, so he started his computer and found that his Internet and e-mail failed to work. He called technical support before 6:00 A.M. and reached a sleepy-sounding person. This young man talked through the problem for a while before he passed off Pat to someone else. Over the next hour and a half, Pat talked to four individuals. Not one knew how to fix his problem.

Eventually, the experts decided that an electrical spike must have fried something. So they scheduled an on-site tech to come out the next day.

The next morning the doorbell rang. Pat expected a technical support person, so you can imagine his surprise when he opened the door to find pop singer Elton John. When Pat looked more closely, he thought, *That can't be Elton because I don't think Elton has a nose ring.* The Elton look-alike introduced himself as Tim.

Pat invited Tim in, and Tim replaced the cable modem. Not only that, but Tim also found an additional problem outside the house, so he scheduled an outside tech for the next day. Pat had an opportunity to talk with Tim a little about his life and then gave him an autographed copy of *The Man in the Mirror.*

Tim left, and Pat turned on the computer. Nothing. After Pat crawled underneath his desk, he discovered that Tim had disconnected every wire to and from the computer and had even unplugged the power source. Pat had no idea where any of the wires went.

The next morning Pat heard a knock and went downstairs and opened the door. Standing in front of him appeared the largest head of dreadlocks he had ever seen. They belonged to a very nice young man who worked on outside wiring.

After he finished his work, he and Pat got into a deep and meaningful spiritual conversation. Pat asked him how he was doing, and he said, "I'm doing pretty good, except for one lifelong problem."

"Well, what's that?" Pat asked.

"Well, life itself," the young man replied.

"Tell me about that," Pat asked. So the tech explained some of the things he had done to try to find happiness.

"Are you a reader?" Pat wondered.

"Yeah, I am doing a little reading," the man answered. "In fact, I'm reading two books right now. One's about the religion of Bob Marley [deceased reggae legend], and the second is the Bible."

Of course, Pat's ears perked up.

"You know," Pat said, "I happen to write books for men, and if you'd be interested, I'd be happy to give you a copy of one of my books." The two ended up having a tremendous conversation. It may have started out as a technological bad-hair day, but it ended up as a great people day!

Pat could easily have looked at those two men, both very different from him, and rejected them without ever giving them a chance. But to follow Christ means that you embrace people, not separate yourself from them.

Where did Pat get this mind-set? He got it from his father. If Pat would have ever made an ethnic, racial, or religious slur while growing up, his father would have slapped him so far across the room he would have needed a road map to get back. His father taught him the importance of respecting all people.

Our children will treat people the way we treat people. How we relate to those who differ from us racially, ethnically, politically, or religiously will no doubt help to create the heritage we pass on to our children.

We started this book by saying that the goal of a father is to disciple the hearts of his children to love God and love others. In this chapter we want to suggest ways you can intentionally lead your children to have a heart that loves people.

FATHERING THE HEART MEANS INSTILLING THE IMPORTANCE OF LOVING OTHERS

No matter what path your children take when they grow up, relationships will remain a huge part of their life. They will have friends, coworkers, neighbors, and often, a spouse and children of their own. The key to these relationships is the ability to love others from the heart.

In John 13:34, Jesus says, "A new command I give you: Love one another." Then he amplifies, "As I have loved you, so you must love one another." In his letter to the Romans, Paul writes, "May our dependably steady and warmly personal God develop maturity in you so that you get along with each other as well as Jesus gets along with us all" (Romans 15:5 THE MESSAGE).

Julian the Apostate is reported to have said of the early Christians, "Those impious Christians. They support not only their own poor, but ours too!" He could resist everything except their love. In our "me-first, fast-paced, online, happiness-now" culture, we find that kind of selfless love in short supply. This shortage presents a great opportunity for Christians.

We suggest you teach your children that if they want to distinguish themselves and stand out from the crowd, they can do so by obeying Jesus' command to love others. Rubin "Hurricane" Carter, the boxer, found himself wrongfully imprisoned for murder. A small group worked to win his release. Soon its members started to develop close relationships. The process dragged on for many years, and Carter believed he needed to stay strong so he could do his time. He finally told those trying to help him, "Do not weaken me with your love." Help your children understand that the most powerful force in the world is love.

Rick and Janine don't know Jesus Christ, but their grown daughter Sandra attends church and a home group with a few other couples. When Rick entered the hospital for bypass surgery, members of Sandra's group came to visit. They also coordinated meals for the family during his recovery. One day as Janine rode in the car with her daughter, she turned to Sandra and said, "I honestly don't understand why your friends have gone out of their way to be so helpful to us. Why do you think that is?"

Sandra gladly told her mom that Jesus' love compels his followers to love others. Rick and Janine actually considered attending church for the first time in many years.

FATHERING THE HEART MEANS TEACHING CHILDREN TO BE OTHERISH

When Jesus tells us to love one another, what is he really asking us to do?

We find a great definition of love in Philippians 2:3: "In humility consider others better than yourselves." In Ephesians 5:25, God commands husbands to love their wives "just as Christ loved the church and gave himself up for her."

Love actively works for someone else's good rather than its own. When you love someone, you feel naturally concerned for what they want and what seems best for them. Your personal interests recede to the background as you promote the interests of another.

As a freshman in college, David woke up every morning and asked himself, "Self, what do you want to do today?" Besides attending class and getting his schoolwork done, every hour seemed fair game for whatever David wanted to do: play basketball, hang out in the dorm, throw the Frisbee, or go to Pete's Restaurant for chicken fingers and French fries. So every day David did pretty much whatever he wanted to do—in a word, *selfish*.

All that changed his sophomore year when he met Ruthie. Instead of waking up and saying, "What do I want to do today?" David woke up and asked, "I wonder what Ruthie is going to do today? I wonder what we could do together?" We call this *otherish*.

We suggest you model "otherishness" to your children. Show them by your own actions that love focuses on the other person. Teach them that love cares about the welfare of others. Help them understand that the way of love thinks about the other person before it thinks about oneself.

Ironically, God has wired us so that when we look out for someone else's interests, we end up satisfying the deepest desires of our own hearts. When our children give themselves to others, they find more joy, peace, and meaning than they could in any other way.

Tom skipped the fishing trip with his buddies to help his youth group reroof the house of a widow in the congregation. He felt tired at the end of the day, but he also had a joyful heart. Elizabeth invited the new girl to sit with her in the cafeteria, even though some of Elizabeth's friends already had said they didn't like her. After lunch, Elizabeth knew deep in her soul she had done the right thing.

This is why the passage on marriage in Ephesians goes on to say, "He who loves his wife loves himself" (Ephesians 5:28). A husband who loves his wife loves himself. The most "selfish" thing a husband could do—the thing that will bring him the most joy—is to deny his own desires and sacrificially love his wife. As Jesus said, "Whoever loses his life for me will find it" (Matthew 16:25). The most "selfish" thing our children can do is to be "otherish" and love others above themselves.

Barriers to Loving Others

Why do children have trouble loving others? We could compile quite a list of sinful attitudes: selfishness, pride, an unforgiving spirit, laziness, low self-esteem, judgmentalism, and more. And that's to say nothing about the annoying and ruthless things that other kids can do to them! Where do these attitudes come from, and how can our children overcome them? Put yourself into some everyday situations:

- New neighbors move in across the street. In your first few interactions they seem gruff and distant. What does it feel like to reach out to a grumpy person you don't know?
- A coworker's father dies after an excruciating battle with cancer. She returns to work after the funeral. How does it feel the first time you speak to her and have no idea what to say?
- In a meeting, a member of your team argues that a crucial mistake has been made on the project—and then blames you. You feel every eye in the room turn to you as he finishes speaking. What emotions do you feel?

These situations can scare us. They can frustrate us. They can make even an adult feel a deep ache in the pit of his or her stomach. Imagine, then, what it's like for a child! Our children face similar decisions every day about whether to love others or look out for themselves.

Teach your kids that love carries real risks. They may suffer in the short run. If they make an effort to reach out to someone new, they run the risk of rejection. If they speak to a hurting person when they don't know exactly what to say, they risk feeling foolish or awkward. When they get in a conflict with others or are accused of a mistake, they will feel as though they have to win in order to be happy. And when they do let someone else win, it will often feel like a loss.

So what will motivate them to take the risk to love? They will love with abandon only after they've felt what it's like to be loved with abandon. Your children need an absolute assurance of the love of Christ before they will have the freedom to truly love others. You can help them gain this assurance by showing them the unconditional love of Christ through your own love. Tell them every day, "I love you," and, "I'm proud of you." Pray that Jesus will so fill their emotional tanks with his love that they will have plenty of love for themselves and enough left over to share with others.

How You Can Help Your Children Love Others

Consider a few practical steps to help equip your children to get along better with different types of people.

Lead a family Bible study on Romans 12:9–21. Begin by meditating on this passage for several days. Consider the traits it describes. Ask yourself, "Do I see this in my own life? Do I see my children growing in this area? What can I do to instill this attitude in them?" Journal your thoughts, and after a few days meet with your children to talk about what the passage teaches and how you might apply it in your family. Consider preparing studies from five angles for five days.

> Love must be sincere. Hate what is evil; cling to what is good. Be devoted to one another in brotherly love. Honor one another above yourselves. Never be lacking in zeal, but keep your spiritual fervor, serving the Lord. Be joyful in hope, patient in affliction, faithful in prayer. Share with God's people who are in need. Practice hospitality.

> Bless those who persecute you; bless and do not curse. Rejoice with those who rejoice; mourn with those who mourn. Live in harmony with one another. Do not be proud, but be willing to associate with people of low position. Do not be conceited.

> Do not repay anyone evil for evil. Be careful to do what is right in the eyes of everybody. If it is possible, as far as it depends

on you, live at peace with everyone. Do not take revenge, my friends, but leave room for God's wrath, for it is written: "It is mine to avenge; I will repay," says the Lord. On the contrary:

"If your enemy is hungry, feed him;
    if he is thirsty, give him something to drink.
In doing this, you will heap burning coals on his head."

Do not be overcome by evil, but overcome evil with good.

Romans 12:9–21

Listen to how Eugene Peterson translates three of these verses: "Get along with each other; don't be stuck-up. Make friends with nobodies; don't be the great somebody. Don't hit back; discover beauty in everyone. If you've got it in you, get along with everybody" (Romans 12:16–18 THE MESSAGE).

Serve others in tangible ways, and allow your children to take part. Tim and Janice make a habit of opening their home two Sunday nights a month for dinner or dessert to show hospitality and make new friends. Bob and Karen host a home Bible study each week. Frank and Julie serve in the care ministry at their church and often take meals to people in crisis. Eric is a single father who helps with the homeless ministry at his church.

Your children will observe all of these tangible efforts to love others and begin to absorb the mentality themselves. As they see your life blessed through service, they will realize the way to go up is to go down.

Make a habit of consciously laying aside your agenda to help others. David's wife, Ruthie, stays in touch with several women who are going through crises. You can't schedule a crisis, and often they don't happen at the most convenient times. When something comes up at night, David puts the kids to bed and allows Ruthie to meet with her friends.

Lay a foundation with your kids every day that they are important to you and high on your agenda. (Make sure you don't help others while ignoring your kids.) If you keep this in balance, then when they see you sacrifice for others, they will learn a powerful lesson. It doesn't mean they will always like it! On more than one occasion David's children have said, "Why can't Mommy just stay home with us tonight instead of helping someone else?" Still, David and Ruthie can already see the same servant spirit growing in their children.

Consciously help your children develop relationships with all types of people. Children are born self-absorbed and in most cases don't like change. Add to this the fact that most adults enjoy being around people similar to them, and it can lead to insulated children who learn to relate only to certain types of people.

Enroll them in sports and activities where they can meet children different from themselves. Pat and Patsy took their children to municipal track meets where they rubbed shoulders with inner-city kids. Get involved in community initiatives where you can experience diversity. Teach them how to behave at a formal dinner. Take them to your favorite hole-in-the-wall restaurant and let them meet the cook. Host a foreign-study student in your home. Serve a meal at a homeless shelter. Expose them to as many different types of people as you can. When their children were young, Pat and Patsy actively involved them in Pat's ministry of racial reconciliation.

FATHERING THE HEART MEANS SWIMMING UPSTREAM

We have a lot to overcome to help our children love others. Unlike Eastern culture, where the good of the community takes center stage, American culture focuses on what's good for the individual. Our educational system, the media, advertisers, and even employers clamor for us to think about ourselves and put our own needs first. In a society like this, relationships with other people become only a means to attain our goals.

When we pray the Lord's Prayer (see Matthew 6:9–13), we say, "*Our* Father." Why not "*My* Father"? We say, "Give *us* today." Why not "Give *me* today"? The Bible insists that God created us to exist in relationships with others. The Bible consistently presents a community perspective. God himself exists in relationship: three persons in one. The Father, Son, and Holy Spirit exist in an eternal love relationship with one another. Being made in the image of God means that we, too, were made for relationships with God and others.

When we are in Christ, the Bible says we become part of a new community—the new people of God in the kingdom of God. We have a new identity because we have become part of the family of God. If we don't equip our children to love others as a core value, they will miss something essential about who they are in Christ.

FATHERING THE HEART REMINDS US THAT LOVING OTHERS CHANGES THE WORLD

Damien de Veuster was born in the middle of the nineteenth century to Belgian farmers. After completing his education, he became a priest and joined the Fathers of the Sacred Hearts. His order sent him as a missionary to Hawaii, where he arrived in 1865.

The increasing numbers of Europeans traveling to Hawaii at the time brought new diseases for which the natives had no immunity: smallpox, influenza, cholera, and, most dreaded of all, leprosy. In 1868, the Hawaiian government established a leper colony on the island of Molokai in an attempt to contain the spread of the disease.

During the next five years the government sent nearly one thousand lepers to the colony. The stark conditions—no houses, no facilities—forced the lepers to take shelter in caves or under trees. No one from the government or health department dared live in the colony.

Father Damien lived in Kohala, but he began to think more and more about the lepers on Molokai. The love of Christ compelled him. In May 1873, Father Damien's superiors approved his request to move his ministry to the leper settlement.

When he arrived, Father Damien took shelter under a large tree. The human disfigurement and the smell of rotting flesh overwhelmed his senses. But he believed God had called him to love these people. He began to meet their physical needs, changing their bandages and treating their wounds. A skilled carpenter himself, he taught them how to build houses. The lepers eventually built a large chapel, where Father Damien held services.

From the start, Father Damien knew he would inevitably get leprosy. He reconciled himself to this fact and faithfully served the people of the leper colony for almost sixteen years until his own death in April 1889. Father Damien has received honor throughout the world for his compassion, courage, and love. His bronze figure resides in the statuary hall in Washington, D.C.

What kind of father did Damien have? Surely, the seed of Damien's love for others found good soil within him, but it takes a father to make this kind of love grow. What would happen if our generation of fathers could grow one hundred men and women like Father Damien? What about one thousand? What about ten thousand? The answer is simple: We would change the world.

From where will the next Father Damien come? Make a prayerful commitment right now to father your child's heart to love God and others. If you do, the next Father Damien may be as close as your child's bedroom.

THE HEART OF THE MATTER

- Our children will treat people the way we treat people.
- Fathering the heart means teaching our children to think of others before thinking of themselves.
- Your children will love with abandon only when they have been loved with abandon by you and Christ.
- Fathering the heart means helping our children serve others in tangible ways.
- Fathering the heart means teaching our children to relate to all types of people.
- Because we are made in the image of the triune God, we were made for relationships.

TAKE IT TO HEART
QUESTIONS FOR APPLICATION AND DISCUSSION

1. What forces in our culture cause a child to think about his or her own interests? Which of these do you think has the most powerful influence on your children? Why?

2. Describe an experience where sacrificially loving another person brought you joy and peace. How would you explain this "paradox of the gospel" to your children—that you found your life when you gave it away?

3. What practical step could you take to involve your children in service to others during the next month?

4. Do you believe your children feel that God loves them with abandon? Do they believe you love them this way? Why or why not? What one thing can you do this week to help them experience more of the love of Christ?

STRAIGHT TO THE HEART
Helping Your Children Deal with Disappointment

One night David's son had a hard time going to sleep. He was looking forward to something special the next day—visiting a theme park with some friends. After several false starts, he finally found the words to tell his mother what troubled him. "Whenever I look forward to something," he said, "I picture how it is going to be in my mind. But then when it actually happens, it is nothing like that. I picture it as a 10, but then when it happens, it is only a 2."

It pains us to watch our children deal with heartache, disappointment, and suffering, doesn't it? Yet these disappointments offer a wonderful opportunity to father our children's hearts.

What can we do to help our children learn from times of disappointment?

Allow them to feel the pain. Don't offer platitudes or unwanted advice when your children hurt. Instead, empathize with them and allow them to express how they feel. Listen to them. Or just sit quietly with them as they cry. Sometimes our kids just need a hug.

Help them face reality. When the time is right, talk with your kids about their feelings. Help them understand that the Bible says we will always be disappointed and frustrated in this world because of the Fall. Help them learn that this world is not their home (1 Peter 1:3–9; 2:9–12). Because it is not our home, our hearts will always long for something more. Help them see this truth:

> Therefore we do not lose heart. Though outwardly we are wasting away, yet inwardly we are being renewed day by day. For our light and momentary troubles are achieving for us an eternal glory that far outweighs them all. So we fix our eyes not on what is seen, but on what is unseen. For what is seen is temporary, but what is unseen is eternal.
>
> 2 Corinthians 4:16–18

Point them to a true hope. How easy it is to become complacent and believe that this is all there is! After all, most of us have a pretty good life: air-conditioning, a television set, computer games, and plenty of food. Who needs heaven? Times of disappointment present a great opportunity to point our children to something beyond this present life.

The Bible says that one day God will restore the world to the way he intended it to be. This is a sure hope to grasp during the storms of life. Help your children allow their disappointments to increase their longing for God's kingdom to come (see Romans 8:18–25).

Our children will react to disappointment in one of two ways: They can harden their hearts and fortify themselves against the pain, or they can allow God to soften their hearts as they experience his love and hope in a broken world. Father your children's hearts through times of disappointment so they can love God and others.

CHAPTER 12

Your Heart First,
Then Theirs

In the introduction we promised that this book would not become a list of dos and don'ts that would bury you in an avalanche of guilt. Still, we have given you a tremendous number of principles and practical suggestions about how you can father the hearts of your children.

It wouldn't surprise us if you felt a bit overwhelmed and wondered where to begin. That's a very normal reaction. So what should you do now? If you'll give us permission, in this chapter we'd like to father *your* heart.

In the same way your children's actions flow from their beliefs, the choices you make as a father flow out of your heart. If you have felt convicted or motivated by things you've read in this book, don't begin to change by adding a list of tasks to your to-do list. Instead of asking yourself, "*What* am I doing as a father?" we suggest you ask, "*Why* am I doing the things I am doing as a father?" The place for you to begin is the same place we asked you to begin with your children: Begin with your own heart.

Henry is a man with a plan. He did well in school, married Tina, his college sweetheart, then went to law school. He slogged through the long days and nights and graduated near the top of his class. He went to work in a 400-man firm and did everything they asked. "Everything" included sixty- to seventy-hour weeks for eight years. Meanwhile, he and Tina had three children whom he rarely saw.

Finally, in October all the hard work paid off when he made partner. Professionally, he had everything he ever wanted.

That's why he never saw it coming.

Henry had been in Chicago for three days of taking depositions. He felt tired when he pulled his car into their three-car garage. He opened the door and said, "I'm home." No answer. He walked upstairs, and there in the hallway he saw the children's suitcases, packed and ready to go.

"What's up?" he asked Tina. With a chill that Henry had not seen even from his toughest opponent, Tina told him, "Henry, I'm taking the children and moving in with my mom and dad. I just can't live this way anymore. I gave you my heart, and you abandoned it."

Henry didn't understand. He was in shock. Everything he had done, he did to help Tina and the children. Sure, they sacrificed for his work. But he was the one who got up early and came home late. He had made $115,000 the previous year. This year as a partner he would make $350,000, minimum. Didn't Tina understand what that meant for their family? How could she be so ungrateful?

What am I going to do now? he wondered. *Leaving my job is not really an option, not after working this hard to get where I am. I'll just have to figure out a way to get Tina back.*

Though successful in his work, Henry had lost touch with his heart. He failed to see the price tag he would have to pay for such professional success. Many have fallen into such a trap. Like Elvis sang, "I'm caught in a trap. I can't get out."

Actually, you *can* get out. We'd like to show you how.

FATHERING THE HEART MEANS
UNDERSTANDING YOUR OWN HEART

Many men have lost touch with their hearts. They believe in Jesus, but they do not passionately follow him. Regrettably, they don't feel passionate about anything "big." They would die for the

Green Bay Packers, but their bodies feel like deadweight when they think about prayer or volunteering for a work day at church.

Why would a man surrender his heart to his career, a sports team, a sexual fantasy, or the lethargic routine of watching hours of television every day? We see this every day in our work with men. Men don't want to be dispassionate—it's just that they know only enough about God to feel disappointed with him. These men have not yet experienced (or have forgotten) the power that God releases when we enter the "real presence" of Jesus. Their hearts remain cold because they do not put themselves where hearts get warm.

As a result, they don't have a big enough vision for what God can do. J. Hudson Taylor, the missionary, once said, "Many Christians estimate difficulties in light of their own resources, and thus attempt little and often fail at the little they attempt. All God's giants have been weak men who did great things for God because they reckoned on God being with them."

We need a bigger God. We need to sit in the presence of his gaze. Brother Lawrence, a dishwasher in a monastery in medieval times, said, "I tell you that this sweet and loving gaze of God insensibly kindles a divine fire in the soul which is set ablaze so ardently with the love of God that one is obliged to perform exterior acts to moderate it."[34] Passion is the natural overflow of closeness to and personal relationship with Jesus.

So why do men act out lesser dreams?

FATHERING THE HEART MEANS GOING BEYOND "WHAT?" TO "WHY?"

All men do exactly what they want to do. All our actions flow out of what we believe at that moment will be in our own best interests. Pascal said, "All men seek happiness. This is the motive of every action of every man, even of those who hang themselves."[35]

Even a father who gets up in the middle of the night to take care of a crying baby, and so lets mom sleep, does so because making the sacrifice is what he most wanted to do at the moment—it was the thing that would make him happy. Leo Tolstoy once wrote, "I believe the motive power of all our actions is personal happiness."[36]

All of our actions as fathers come from what's in our hearts. Jesus said, "The things that come out of the mouth come from the heart" (Matthew 15:18). He also taught that "every good tree bears good fruit, but a bad tree bears bad fruit" (Matthew 7:17). Paul praises the Thessalonians for their "work produced by faith, . . . labor prompted by love, and . . . endurance inspired by hope" (1 Thessalonians 1:3). The attitudes and beliefs of our hearts produce our actions. "As [a man] thinketh in his heart, so is he" (Proverbs 23:7 KJV).

When we sin, it means something has gone wrong in our hearts. We don't fully believe something about the gospel of Jesus. When we think we need something "more" or something "else" to satisfy our deepest desires for happiness, we don't fully believe the promises of God. Or we don't think Jesus is enough, so we add to the gospel of Jesus—we add money, success, prestige, or sins of the flesh.

We all do exactly what we want to do. And too often we don't believe Jesus is enough to make us happy. We doubt that his promises can satisfy or bring us joy, peace, meaning, or purpose. This is what the Bible calls unbelief. All sin results from unbelief. Unbelief means looking to something other than Jesus Christ to meet our needs and make us whole.

When Simon grows tired or stressed, he visits websites to look at naked women. Why? Because Simon believes that pornography will deliver something Jesus can't.

Rick works too much. He has consistently missed important family events because of his career. Why? Because Rick believes he won't be happy unless he gets what a successful career can bring.

Alonzo flies off the handle with his children over the least little thing. When they don't do things the way he wants them to, the rage boils inside until he can't hold it in. Why? Because Alonzo wants to control his life and get his own way.

For every one of these men, the sinful action is merely the visible symptom of something going on in their hearts—a lack of faith in the gospel of Jesus.

Performance versus Faith

Eric has great people skills, which earned him a promotion to branch manager of a local bank. The top management recognized his skill and started grooming him for an executive position.

It didn't take long for Eric to discover the things he needed to do to become a success. He learned how to dress appropriately and how to handle himself in meetings. He learned how to introduce himself to the right people. He worked hard to make sure his e-mails, letters, and presentations got done in the most professional manner. And his hard work paid off with promotion after promotion.

Eric got transferred to a small community where most people went to church. The second Sunday after they had moved, he decided to visit a church with his wife. The church didn't seem too bad, so Eric regularly returned. Soon he decided to join the men for a luncheon where a local professional athlete had agreed to speak. As he got more involved, Eric began to subconsciously analyze his new environment the same way he had analyzed his old one.

He quickly realized that he needed to give money to the church to be considered a good member. He joined a small group of men who met early in the morning to read and discuss a book. The church leadership asked him to serve on the finance committee, so he began to attend those monthly meetings. He heard how others prayed when they prayed out loud, and he began to speak the same way in his prayers. Just two years after joining the church, Eric was nominated to be a deacon. Now he had it all. Not only had he achieved success in his career, he had found "success" with God as well.

It doesn't take long for most of us to figure out the requirements for the culture in which we find ourselves. Every church has its own culture. If you raise your hands in a church where people don't raise their hands, you will immediately figure out that it's not "acceptable behavior" and, unless you're very unusual, you'll stop.

We all want to fit in. So a man at church quickly figures out how to dress, which phrases will bring approval, how often he needs to attend to make the "right" people happy, how much money to give, which committees to serve on, and that he needs to join a men's class. Often, we take a man from one performance-oriented culture (the world) and move him right into another (the church).

The problem is that we can substitute our ability to perform for a true heart of faith. We can substitute our own strength for dependence on the gospel of Jesus. We can match our external behavior to the ideals of the culture without actually believing it. We can focus on the fruit and neglect the root.

FATHERING THE HEART MEANS DIGGING UP ROOTS OF SIN, NOT PICKING ORANGES AND TAPING ON APPLES

Many homes where we live in Orlando, Florida, have orange trees in their yards. Imagine you live here, have an orange tree in your yard, and decide you don't want an orange tree anymore. Instead, you want an apple tree. You could go out in the yard and pick every orange off the tree. After that you could get in your car and drive to the store, buy a bagful of apples and duct tape, then come home and tape apples all over the tree.

But what would happen? In a few days the apples would begin to rot, then fall off the trees.

And what would happen next year? The oranges would return. The only way to get rid of the oranges for good is to dig up the tree by its roots.

Too often we simply "pick oranges and tape on apples." We try to remove the bad behavior we see, but we don't get to the root of our unbelief. So even if we can will ourselves to stop some sinful behaviors this season, they come right back because we still have the same root of unbelief.

Christ offers us the chance for change from the roots, from the inside out. He calls us to stop making our ability to perform our god and start walking with him by faith. It's a great life when you don't feel as though you always have to perform to make God happy!

Jesus and Moralism

In John 3, Jesus abruptly cut off Nicodemus's opening words and cryptically told him he needed to be "born again." In the very next chapter, Jesus has an extended conversation with a woman at a well. He talks with the woman freely, yet doesn't seem to let Nicodemus get a word in edgewise. Why?

The woman at the well knew she needed a Savior, so Jesus conversed with her and led her to a correct understanding of his identity. Nicodemus was a moralist who believed that his own efforts made him righteous, so he looked at Jesus as a teacher who could give him a few tips to help him become an even better man. Jesus sounded harsh with Nicodemus because he wanted to rock his world.

If you think God will accept you because of what you do, then you have only one hope: to be "born again." Jesus did not come to help us save ourselves. He's not some self-help guru from a late-night infomercial. He is not a "spiritual personal trainer" who coaches us to become spiritually fit. He is not just a teacher to whom we can look for advice and information. Jesus is a Savior, because a Savior is what we really need.

As Jesus said, "It is not the healthy who need a doctor, but the sick. . . . For I have not come to call the righteous, but sinners" (Matthew 9:12–13). It's okay to admit that you can't handle it on your own and that your heart has failed you. Jesus came to save big sinners like us.

The gospel calls us to renounce our desire to live independent of God and instead instructs us to cling to him by faith. We must forsake all idols—even the idol of our own good works—and worship God alone. We always fail when we try to do what God wants us to do in our own strength. The key is to focus on Christ and allow God's Holy Spirit to transform us so that *we want to do what God wants us to do.*

In chapter 8, "Growing a Heart of Faith in Your Child," we suggested a prayer you could use to confess your faith in Jesus. We have again placed this prayer here. If you have grasped that the gospel is about faith alone in Christ alone and feel ready to surrender to (rather than perform for) Jesus, we encourage you to memorialize your desire by praying and making Jesus your Savior and Lord. This may be the first time you have ever truly surrendered your life, or it may be an act of rededication. In either case, we encourage you to pray . . .

> *Lord Jesus, I need you in my life. I confess that I have been trying to find happiness in impotent and sinful ways. Thank you for dying on the cross to pay the penalty for my sins. More than any other thing, I know that to be happy I need to put my faith solely in you to be my Savior and Lord. I invite you to take control of my life and show me how to live by faith rather than by trying to be good. Amen.*

If you have just prayed, we encourage you to continue learning what "the gospel" really means. Also, we encourage you to build a lifestyle of faith.

We'd also like to ask you to consider this exercise: the next time you become aware of sin in your life, don't focus merely on the behavior. Instead, ask yourself, "What root is bringing forth this fruit?" Pray and ask God to reveal to you what is going on in your heart that led to this behavior. Next, ask him to change you from the inside out. Ask him to show you how destructive these attitudes are and how much joy you can find by turning to him.

COMING FULL CIRCLE

In some ways, we have come full circle and end at the beginning. How could a book on fathering be complete unless it helped you see that all the techniques and tips in the world won't help unless you become the man God wants you to be? We hope you have found the gospel of Jesus. He alone is the way!

Jesus said to the apostle Paul, "My grace is sufficient for you, for my power is made perfect in weakness." Paul's response? "I delight in weaknesses.... For when I am weak, then I am strong" (2 Corinthians 12:9–10).

We pray that you won't try to father your children's hearts in your own strength but rather that you would delight in your inability and humbly trust Christ each step of the way.

THE HEART OF THE MATTER

- Fathering the heart means beginning with our own hearts.
- Many men have lost touch with their hearts and do not feel passionate about anything "big."
- The attitudes and beliefs of our hearts produce our actions.
- When we sin, it means something has gone wrong in our hearts.
- Men often substitute their ability to perform for a true heart of faith.
- We can't have the fruit without the root.
- The Holy Spirit must transform us so that we want to do what God wants us to do.

TAKE IT TO HEART
QUESTIONS FOR DISCUSSION AND APPLICATION

- **Find the fruit:** Identify an area of sin in your life where you have overreacted to outside pressures. (For example, yelling at your children for small things or being defensive with your coworkers.) Write it down or describe it to your group.

- **Uncover the root:** Answer the question, "What causes me to think and feel this way? What do I think this sin will do for me that God can't?" (For example, you may enjoy pornography because you believe you need the thrill and physical pleasure it provides in order to be happy.) Describe your thoughts to the group.

- **Ask God to dig it up:** What promises of the gospel deal with this specific issue? Consider specific passages of Scripture that might apply. Allow other men in your group to help you.

Conclude with group or personal prayer, and ask Jesus to show you his glory and sufficiency and to help you know that only he can satisfy the deepest longings of your heart.

Paying the Price

THE PRICE OF SUCCESS OR THE PRICE OF FAILURE

If you have children, you know there is a price to pay to be a father. Every father will pay the full price of rearing his children—either the price of failure or the price of success. There are no exceptions. This is an iron law.

The price of success must be paid now, today, and it is costly—but the reward will come when hairs turn gray and grandchildren come to play.

The price of failure may be put off to later, tomorrow, but when the note comes due, you reap sorrow unspeakable—child pain, a pain that never goes away. Every child is worth the price his or her father was willing to pay.

Is that it, then? you may wonder. *What about me? Is this all there is?*

If you did not have a father willing to pay the price of your success, fortunately, another Father eagerly paid the full note to buy you back . . . if you will receive it. His Son for your father's son.

Yes, that would be you.

"Father Five"

NOTE: David, a math major, came up with some astonishing statistics, explained below. If you decide to father the hearts of five children during your lifetime—including your own—you will have a profound impact on the future of the world.

America's current fathering system isn't working. It undermines the foundations of our churches and families, and it will have even more devastating consequences in generations to come.

Americans have an average of 2.4 children. With our current fathering system, only 60 percent of children who grow up in church remain active in church as adults. What does this mean in the long run? And how could this change if we can challenge a generation of dads to father the heart?

Assume we begin with a thousand Christians (five hundred married couples). If each couple has 2.4 children and this continues into the future, what happens over the next few generations? Take a look at the following numbers:[37]

	# children	percent Christian as adults	# children	percent Christian as adults
	2.4	60 %	2.4	80 %
Time	# of adult Christians		# of adult Christians	
Start	1,000		1,000	
After Generation 1 (20 years)	720		960	
Generation 2 (40 years)	518		922	
Generation 3 (60 years)	373		885	
Generation 4 (80 years)	269		849	
Generation 5 (100 years)	193		815	
Generation 6 (120 years)	139		783	
Generation 7 (140 years)	100		751	
Generation 8 (160 years)	**72**		**721**	

If things continue as they are now, with Christian couples having 2.4 children and 60 percent of them coming to authentic faith in Christ, then for every thousand Christians now, we will be left with seventy-two Christians after eight generations.

We get a tenfold increase if we can help fathers do better on fathering the heart and only lose 20 percent of our kids (80 percent stick with Christ). But because each father influences only 2.4 children, we will still have only 721 Christians for every thousand Christians now.

What can be done? We'd like to propose "Father Five," an initiative to help Christian dads expand their legacy. We are not suggesting that you need five biological children but rather that you try to intentionally influence at least five children in every generation (every twenty years). "Father Five" means that you actively seek to father the hearts of five children by discipling them to love God and others.

What would happen if five hundred men accepted this call? Take a look at the following table:

	# children *influenced*	percent Christian as adults	# children *influenced*	percent Christian as adults
	5	60 %	5	80 %
Time	# of adult Christians		# of adult Christians	
Start	1,000		1,000	
After Generation 1 (20 years)	1,500		2,000	
Generation 2 (40 years)	2,250		4,000	
Generation 3 (60 years)	3,375		8,000	
Generation 4 (80 years)	5,063		16,000	
Generation 5 (100 years)	7,594		32,000	
Generation 6 (120 years)	11,391		64,000	
Generation 7 (140 years)	17,086		128,000	
Generation 8 (160 years)	**25,629**		**256,000**	

Even if only 60 percent of the children still stick with Christ, we would have over 25,000 adult Christians after eight generations (instead of seventy-two). And if we combine "Father Five" with the concepts of fathering the heart, after eight generations we would have 256,000 adult Christians! In short, we would change the world.

How can you influence five children for Christ in each generation? Besides investing in your own children, you can reach fathers for Jesus Christ, work in a church children's ministry, invest in your own grandchildren, sponsor a child evangelism missionary, sponsor a heart-oriented fathering seminar in your church, coach youth sports through your church, work with a Boy Scout troop, or bring a Man in the Mirror fathering seminar to your church.[38]

There is no shortage of ways you can father the hearts of five children. The real question is, "What would it take for you to make this a priority?" Consider one reason why we think it would be worth your investment.

THE STORY OF LA FAYETTE SCALES

La Fayette Scales's father, Ralph, served faithfully as a deacon in his church. When La Fayette was seven, doctors diagnosed his father with stomach cancer. Ralph died less than a year later, creating a difficult and lonely time for La Fayette, his brother, and his sister.

After the funeral, the deacons of the church came to La Fayette and his siblings and said, "Ralph Scales was our friend. We are so sorry that your father won't be here anymore. But we want you to know that you will never be alone in this life." And then these men followed through on their kind words.

Calvin Ward, who sang in the choir, started a Sunday school class for the boys. He taught La Fayette how to pray. He held him accountable to reading his Bible every day. He taught La Fayette how to walk in the Holy Spirit.

Deacon Burton didn't have any sons, so when it came time for the father-son banquet each year, he called La Fayette and his brother, Phillip. "Come on, boys. You are my sons tonight. We are going to the banquet."

Harold Shank served as the head of the usher board. When he saw that La Fayette had grown tall and awkward, he took him aside. He recruited La Fayette to be an usher and showed him how to walk confidently with long strides, how to hold his head up high, how to look someone in the eye when he spoke, and how to shake a man's hand with a firm, strong grip.

Wallace Wyatt and Al Walker started a Boy Scout troop at the church. They recruited La Fayette and told him every man needs a code. They took the boys camping in the heat of summer and the cold of winter. They didn't let them off the hook and told them a man has to learn to endure what life brings. They inspired La Fayette to always do better. La Fayette became only the third African-American Eagle Scout in Columbus, Ohio.

These men were not doctors, lawyers, or CEOs. They were factory workers, construction workers, and military personnel. Not many of them even had a college degree, but they did have a vision. They knew that young men need spiritual fathers. They knew that if they invested in a child, they could change the world.

Today, the Reverend La Fayette Scales pastors the Rhema Christian Center, one of the largest churches in Columbus, Ohio. His ministry is not only transforming the city, but he has also touched tens of thousands of people throughout the world. La Fayette is who he is today because of the men who invested in his life. He in turn is leaving a legacy in the lives of thousands of men and children of the next generation.

What would have happened had these men not been spiritual fathers to La Fayette? We don't know, but we're sure glad we'll never have to find out.

We would like to challenge you to "Father Five." Will you accept the challenge? Who knows? The life you touch may be the next La Fayette Scales. Ping us with an e-mail and let us know if you accept at:

fatherfive@maninthemirror.org

A Letter to a Young Man on Interviewing for a Job

NOTE: When Pat's son, John, graduated from college, he asked Pat for advice on how to interview successfully. Pat wrote him the following letter. Feel free to use or adapt this when your sons or daughters want to start working—even part-time jobs while still in high school.

Dear Son,

You asked if I had any interviewing advice for you. I responded, "Just be yourself." I said that partly because you are who you are (no sense making them think they're hiring someone else!) but mostly because you are exactly the kind of man any thinking person would leap to hire!

In the meantime, I recalled how much time I've spent going through interviews, and what has been important. It got me thinking about you, your friends, and the graduating children of men I know. So I decided to write these thoughts for any person who wants to have a good interview.

GETTING READY FOR THE INTERVIEW

Look nice, be nice. You don't have to look like a banker (your interviewer knows you are a student!), but how you present yourself will send a message. The questions are, "What message do I want my appearance to send?" and, "What will make the best impression?" Borrow a coat and tie if you need to.

Hop on the Web and *check out the company*. Sprinkle your conversation with a couple of company facts, and watch the interviewer warm to you.

Prepare. You have plenty of things to think about in advance. Do so, but then try not to think much about it on the actual day of your interview.

Relax. Don't interview right after a high-stress exam, after an all-nighter, or on the day a paper is due. Instead, plan some chill time and a good night's rest.

Pray. Ask God for wisdom and clarity of thought. Ask him to animate you and help you make a positive impression. Ask the Holy Spirit to fill you with power and purpose. Tell God of your willingness to submit this interview to the sovereign pleasure and purpose of his will.

Be ten minutes early. Punctuality is one of the biggest problems in the work world. Besides, if you're cutting it too close, you'll just make yourself nervous (and you're going to be nervous enough already).

FIRST IMPRESSIONS

Establish eye contact. Look your interviewer in the eye, especially as you first shake hands. As for your wet hand—don't worry too much. It won't be the first time your interviewer has shaken a damp hand. (Still, wipe your hand discreetly just before you go in.) And about that handshake—be firm and confident.

Smile often. Smiles warm up a room—and the people in the room. You'll feel nervous, so you'll have to concentrate on making this happen. Hint: Use any mentions of the company, a mentor or teacher, your parents, or any loved one as "triggers" to remind you to smile.

DURING THE INTERVIEW ITSELF

Early in the interview find out *how long the interview will last*. This will help you to pace yourself. Also, after the first couple of questions it may be a good idea to ask your interviewer, "Are my answers about the right length, or should I give you more or less?" This will be appreciated—nothing is more frustrating than talking to someone whose answers are too brief or are "TMI" (too much information).

Be sure to have plenty of *ongoing eye contact.* Research shows that the speaker normally makes eye contact about 60 percent of the time. When the interviewer talks, look into his or her eyes nearly 100 percent of the time. It's very distracting to talk to someone who isn't looking at you.

Think of four or five good questions that will help you understand the company, and ask them in the interview. (Write them down if you want.) Ask questions that show interest in what you can do for the company rather than what they can do for you. For example, don't ask, "Are there benefits?" until after you've been offered a job. Do ask questions like these:

- What is the history, long-term vision, and mission of the company?
- What are the values of the company?
- How long have you been with the company, and what do you like most about it?
- Where do you think I could make a contribution?

WHAT YOUR INTERVIEWER WILL BE LOOKING FOR

Chemistry and *competence.* Or, if you prefer, *personality* and *performance.* These are the two sides of the employment seesaw. Employers want likable people who can get the job done.

The company you are interviewing has a *mission,* probably in writing. They are trying to find someone who will be a "getter-doner" and a team player. They are interested in hiring someone for their reasons, not yours.

Here are a few questions you may be asked:

- What are your ambitions?
- Why do you think you would be suited for this position?
- What are your strengths and weaknesses?

Don't assume your interviewer has even read *your résumé*, much less remembered anything on it. Make a list of *five, six, or seven points* you really want to get across, then memorize it. Perhaps an acrostic to help you remember? Don't oversell yourself, but don't undersell yourself either.

POSSIBLE POINTS TO INCLUDE

Your ability to get things done. Give an example of how you finished a complicated school or extracurricular project while maintaining other responsibilities. Employers want to see the "signals" of a strong work ethic.

Your willingness to learn and take direction. They are not looking for a twenty-two-year-old to come in and help them restructure the company. They want someone who will work hard, wants to grow, and will follow directions. Give an example of how you have done this as a son/daughter or as a student.

Your attention to detail and follow-through. If you have it, they will want it—so tell them. If you have an organized mind, give an example of a project that required you to juggle a lot of balls.

Your major accomplishments. You may get a question like, "What are your major accomplishments?" Be prepared to share milestones that required grit and tenacity. Did you have a job during college? Work it in.

Your ability to work with and get along with people (signals: team player, management potential). Tell them about how you chaired a committee that helped elect the Student Government Association president or about how you organized a study group.

Your attitude and character. Contrary to anything you may have heard, the foundation of business is integrity and trust. Your character is key to success—meaning what you say, delivering on your promises, and being dependable. Let them know your personal values.

Be as concrete and specific as possible. For example, don't say, "I am willing to learn and take direction." Instead, give them an example of how you have learned a difficult skill or subject, or how you learned to take direction from a coach. Don't get bogged down trying to think of "everything." Instead, pick your best points and leave it at that.

Curve Balls

Sometimes I will ask an off-the-wall question in the middle of an interview just to see how an interviewee thinks on his or her feet. One example for me is, "How do you keep score?" Or, "Who is the most interesting person you have ever met, and why?" Or, "What kind of people annoy you most?" Don't let a question like this throw you. Pause for a moment and, as a friend once suggested to me, say the *second* thing that comes to mind.

I have two questions I like to ask near the end of the interview. Chances are you won't get asked either one, but you ought to be ready just in case you are. First, "What else should I have asked you?" Second, "Is there anything else you would like to ask me?"

The Secret Weapon

The most successful employees are the ones who take their jobs *personally* (technically we would call this *conscientiousness*). Tell your interviewer, "If you select me for this position, you can be sure that I will take it personally. It won't be just a job."

Ending the Interview

Be prepared to end at the appointed time, but let your interviewer do the ending. The interviewer will probably mention a "next step." But if they don't, be sure to say something like, "I'm very interested in pursuing this. Where do we go from here?" or, "I really appreciate this opportunity to learn more about your company. What is the next step?"

BE YOURSELF

You'll do super by being who you already are. So relax as much as you can, and have fun! God's will be done.

I love you and am so proud of you,

Dad

APPENDIX 3

Recommended Resources

Chapman, Gary, and Ross Campbell, M.D. *The Five Love Languages of Children.* Chicago: Northfield Publishers, 1997.

Dobson, James. *Bringing Up Boys.* Wheaton, Ill.: Tyndale House, 2001.

Jones, Stan, and Brenna Jones. *Facing the Facts.* God's Design for Sex series. Colorado Springs: NavPress, 1994.

_____. *What's the Big Deal?* God's Design for Sex series. Colorado Springs: NavPress, 1994

Lewis, Robert. *Raising a Modern-Day Knight: A Father's Role in Guiding His Son to Authentic Manhood.* Colorado Springs: Focus on the Family Publishing, 1997.

Miller, C. John, and Barbara Miller Juliani. *Come Back, Barbara.* 2d ed. Phillipsburg, N.J.: P&R Publishing, 1997.

Morley, Patrick. *The Young Man in the Mirror: A Rite of Passage into Manhood.* Nashville: Broadman & Holman, 2003.

Nystrom, Carolyn. *Before I Was Born.* God's Design for Sex series. Colorado Springs: NavPress, 1991.

Packer, J. I. *Concise Theology.* Wheaton, Ill.: Tyndale House, 1993.

Tripp, Paul David. *Age of Opportunity: A Biblical Guide to Parenting Teens.* 2d ed. Phillipsburg, N.J.: P&R Publishing, 2001.

Tripp, Tedd. *Shepherding a Child's Heart.* Wapwallopen, Pa.: Shepherd Press, 2001.

Website: http://www.heritagebuilders.com

Dads' Discussion Group Leader's Guide

One of the best ways to use this book is in a group study with other men. The combined wisdom and insight of the group will help you apply to your life the truths you read. The men can also help answer questions and encourage you in areas of difficulty or neglect.

Consider the following ideas to help you begin a group:

STARTING A NEW GROUP

Photocopy this book's table of contents (pages 7–10) and the questions at the end of a couple of chapters, and give a copy to the men with whom you want to meet. Ask them if they would like to meet with other men, read the book, and answer the discussion questions at the end of each chapter. The optimum size for a group is six to eight men (since one or two will end up being absent occasionally).

FIRST WEEK

Distribute a copy of the book to each man. Assign the first chapter as the reading assignment for next week. Ask the men to preview the questions at the end of the chapter and to be prepared to answer them with the group. Close each meeting with five or ten minutes of prayer. Always end when you said you would, since your group members may have appointments to keep.

TYPICAL WEEK

Begin with an ice-breaker question or ask someone (a different person each week) to share his personal testimony in five minutes or less. Then spend forty-five minutes or so discussing the chapter, and close with ten minutes of prayer.

LEADING A DISCUSSION

The key to a successful group is making sure that each man knows that you care about him personally. Allow each man to get "airtime." If someone rambles too much, privately ask him to help draw out the shier members of the group. Keep the discussion on topic as much as possible, but also allow the men to deal with the things they struggle with. You don't have to be an experienced Bible teacher to lead a discussion group. If someone asks a question and you don't know the answer, just say so and move on.

We would like to encourage you to prayerfully consider starting a group rather than reading this book alone. Not only will it enrich your life, it could change the lives of another man's family for generations to come.

Notes

1. Janet G. Woititz, "The 13 Characteristics of Adult Children" (on the Web at http://www.drjan.com/13char.html).
2. Howard Hendricks has said that four out of five children will drop out of church by the time they graduate from high school. Jay Strack says his research indicates an even higher number. As far as long-term impact, Barna reports that only 61 percent of people who attend church as children remain there as adults (see http://www.barna.org/cgi-bin/PagePressRelease.asp?PressReleaseID=101&Reference=C).
3. Paul Schervish, "The New Philanthropists," *The Boston Globe* (2 March 2002), D8.
4. See A. N. W. Saunders, translator, *Greek Political Oratory* (New York: Penguin, 1970).
5. See appendix 1 for a powerful summary of our current situation and prospects for future revival.
6. This table is based in part on the work of Dr. Rod Cooper.
7. *Merriam-Webster's Collegiate Dictionary*, "folly" (Springfield, Mass.: Merriam-Webster, 1999), 453.
8. Patrick Morley, *Coming Back to God* (Grand Rapids: Zondervan, 2001), 128.
9. See James Dobson, *Bringing Up Boys* (Wheaton, Ill.: Tyndale House, 2001), 107.
10. Olivia Barker, "Why Freak Dancing Freaks Out Schools," *USA Today* (1 June 2001), 1A–2A.
11. The teenage years don't have to be this way, of course. A great resource to help during these years is Paul David Tripp's *Age of Opportunity: A Biblical Guide to Parenting Teens*, 2d ed. (Phillipsburg, N.J.: P&R Publishing, 2001).
12. For a detailed discussion of spiritual gifts see Pat's book, *Discipleship for the Man in the Mirror* (Grand Rapids: Zondervan, 1998), "Developing a

Personal Ministry" (chapter 18); to see a brief article on the subject, log on to http://www.maninthemirror.org, go to "A Look in the Mirror" archives, and select issue #4, "How to Determine Your Spiritual Gifts." Also, Pat's book for high school boys, *The Young Man in the Mirror* (Nashville: Broadman & Holman, 2003), "Becoming Independent" (chapter 11), discusses a child's design, natural abilities, and spiritual gifts from a teenager's point of view.

13. Robert Lewis, *Raising a Modern-Day Knight: A Father's Role in Guiding His Son to Authentic Manhood* (Colorado Springs: Focus on the Family Publishing, 1997).

14. Howard Gardner, *Frames of Mind: The Theory of Multiple Intelligences*, 10th ed. (New York: BasicBooks, 1993). This summary is adapted from Pat's book *The Young Man in the Mirror*.

15. Neil Postman, "Learning by Story," *The Atlantic Monthly* (December 1989), 122–24.

16. Adapted from Neil Postman and Mardi Keyes, "Who Invented Adolescence?" (Rochester, Minn.: Ransom Fellowship, 1994).

17. Patrick Morley, *Coming Back to God* (Grand Rapids: Zondervan, 2001).

18. C. S. Lewis, *Mere Christianity* (San Francisco: HarperSanFrancisco, 2001, reprint; first published, 1952), 136–37.

19. There are a number of helpful resources for laypeople that explain the Christian story. See Patrick Morley, *Coming Back to God* (Grand Rapids: Zondervan, 2001); Lee Strobel, *The Case for Christ* (Grand Rapids: Zondervan, 1998); and Lee Strobel, *The Case for Faith* (Grand Rapids: Zondervan, 2000).

20. For a great resource to gain a better understanding of these and other theological truths, see J. I. Packer, *Concise Theology* (Wheaton, Ill.: Tyndale House, 1993).

21. See Barna press release (http://www.barna.org/cgi-bin/ PagePressRelease.asp?PressReleaseID=101&Reference=C).

22. Patrick Morley, *Seven Seasons of the Man in the Mirror* (Grand Rapids: Zondervan, 1997), 99–100.

23. Paraphrased from Blaise Pascal, *Pensées*, #131 (London: Penguin Books, 1966).

24. Great resources for family devotions can be found at your local Christian bookstore or on the Web (log on to http://www.heritagebuilders.com).

25. Cited in Ron Stodghill, "Where'd You Learn That?" *Time* (15 June 1998), 54.

26. There are many issues of sexuality beyond the scope of this chapter. If you or your wife are the victims of sexual abuse, a helpful resource may be *The Wounded Heart: Hope for Adult Victims of Childhood Sexual Abuse*, by Dr. Dan Allender (Colorado Springs: NavPress, 1990). If you are

struggling with addiction to pornography or other sexual activities, consider the resource *False Intimacy: Understanding the Struggle of Sexual Addiction* by Dr. Harry Schaumburg (Colorado Springs: NavPress, 1997, revised edition). Also, see our article "Conquering a Secret Thought Life," in "A Look in the Mirror" #7 (available on the Web at http://www.maninthemirror.org/alm/alm7.htm).

27. A helpful resource for this are the four books in the God's Design for Sex series published by NavPress: Carolyn Nystrom, *Before I Was Born*, 1991; Stan and Brenna Jones, *The Story of Me*, 1994; Stan and Brenna Jones, *What's the Big Deal?* 1994; Stan and Brenna Jones, *Facing the Facts*, 1994.

28. We believe Onan's sin in Genesis 38 was his not fulfilling his obligation to his brother to produce an heir for his family line.

29. See James Dobson, *Bringing Up Boys* (Wheaton, Ill.: Tyndale, 2001), 78–80.

30. Pat's book *The Young Man in the Mirror* has chapters on sex and dating that include frank and thorough answers to sex and dating questions for high school boys.

31. Summarized from C. John Miller and Barbara Miller Juliani, *Come Back, Barbara*, 2d ed. (Phillipsburg, N.J.: P&R Publishing, 1997).

32. Miller and Juliani, *Come Back, Barbara*, 119.

33. Cited in Charles Swindoll, *You and Your Child* (Nashville: Nelson, 1977), 33–34.

34. Brother Lawrence, *The Practice of the Presence of God* (New York: Doubleday, 1977), 108.

35. Blaise Pascal, *Pensées*, #425 (London: Penguin Books, 1966).

36. Leo Tolstoy, *Anna Karenina*, reissue ed. (New York: Penguin Books, 2001).

37. These charts are for demonstration purposes only. They do not take into account adult conversions, believers married to unbelievers, and so on. But they do provide a general idea of what God could do through men committed to passing their faith to the next generation.

38. For information about how to reach men or about a seminar that deals with fathering the heart, visit Man in the Mirror on the Web at http://www.maninthemirror.org or call 888-MIRROR-1.

Want to read more by Patrick Morley?

A Patrick Morley Reading Guide for Men

Want to Reinvent Yourself?

Want a Success That Really Matters?

Personal Reflections

Man in the Mirror Workbook

For Men in Transition

Practical Direction

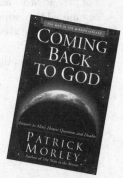

A Compelling Evangelism Tool

Want a Deeper Walk with God?

Practical Theology

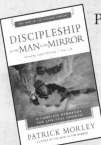

Devotional

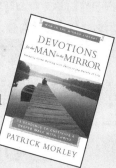

For You

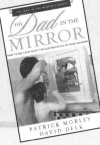

Want a Stronger Family?

For Her

For Both of You

For Son

Solving the 24 Problems Men Face

THE MAN IN THE MIRROR

PATRICK M. MORLEY
Foreword by R.C. Sproul

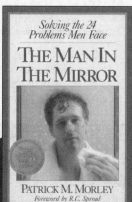

Want to help the men of your church disciple the hearts of their children?

This dynamic event gives men the encouragement and practical insights they need to succeed as Christian fathers. This fun, interactive event engages men both intellectually and emotionally with Biblical truth. This could be the event that God uses to help your men become Dads that make a difference for eternity.

Want to to be a leader who disciples the hearts of men?

Biblical, time-tested strategies "perfectly designed" to produce changed lives, families, churches, and communities. Build a discipling ministry to men that will last and change your church and community forever.

About the Authors

A respected authority on the unique challenges and opportunities men face, Patrick Morley has authored twelve books and 140 articles for and about men. In 1989 he wrote *The Man in the Mirror*, a landmark book that poured from his own search for purpose and a deeper relationship with God. He is the CEO of Man in the Mirror, Inc., and the president of the National Coalition of Men's Ministries (www.ncmm.org). Every Friday morning Patrick teaches a Bible study to 150 businessmen in Orlando, Florida. Audio and video webcasts of these Bible studies are available at no charge (log on to www.maninthemirror.org). He and his wife, Patsy, have two married children.

David Delk is the president of Man in the Mirror, the author of the novel, *Twists of Fate*, and a visiting lecturer at Reformed Theological Seminary. David coauthored four men's seminars, including *Success That Matters*, and is a key faculty member of Man in the Mirror's National Training Center for Men's Evangelism and Discipleship. A sought-after speaker, David loves communicating to the hearts of men the great adventure of following Jesus Christ. Before joining Man in the Mirror, David was a senior consultant to large public utilities with Energy Management Associates. He lives with his wife and three children in Orlando, Florida.

We'd love your feedback! Contact us at
dadinthemirror@maninthemirror.org
or come visit us the next time you're in Orlando!

We want to hear from you. Please send your comments about this book to us in care of zreview@zondervan.com. Thank you.

GRAND RAPIDS, MICHIGAN 49530 USA

WWW.ZONDERVAN.COM